Praxis II

Fundamental Subjects: Content Knowledge Practice Questions

Praxis II Practice Tests & Exam Review for the
Praxis II: Subject Assessments

Dear Future Exam Success Story:

First of all, **THANK YOU** for purchasing Mometrix study materials!

Second, congratulations! You are one of the few determined test-takers who are committed to doing whatever it takes to excel on your exam. **You have come to the right place.** We developed these practice tests with one goal in mind: to deliver you the best possible approximation of the questions you will see on test day.

Standardized testing is one of the biggest obstacles on your road to success, which only increases the importance of doing well in the high-pressure, high-stakes environment of test day. Your results on this test could have a significant impact on your future, and these practice tests will give you the repetitions you need to build your familiarity and confidence with the test content and format to help you achieve your full potential on test day.

Your success is our success

We would love to hear from you! If you would like to share the story of your exam success or if you have any questions or comments in regard to our products, please contact us at **800-673-8175** or **support@mometrix.com**.

Thanks again for your business and we wish you continued success!

Sincerely,
The Mometrix Test Preparation Team

TABLE OF CONTENTS

Practice Test #1

1. Research indicates that developing oral language proficiency in emergent readers is important because:

    a. Proficiency with oral language enhances students' phonemic awareness and increases vocabulary

    b. The more verbally expressive emergent readers are, the more confident they become. Such students will embrace both Academic and Independent reading levels

    c. It encourages curiosity about others. With strong oral language skills, students begin to question the world around them. The more they ask, the richer their background knowledge

    d. It demonstrates to students that their ideas are important and worth sharing

2. Arthur writes a paper. One classmate identifies ideas and words that resonated with her when she read it. Another describes how reading the paper changed his thinking. A third asks Arthur some questions about what he meant by certain statements in the paper. A fourth suggests a portion of the paper that needs more supporting information. This description is most typical of...

    a. A portfolio assessment.

    b. A holistic scoring.

    c. A scoring rubric.

    d. A peer review.

3. Which text should a teacher choose in order to practice the skills of previewing and reviewing information?

    a. A poem

    b. A chapter from the students' science class textbook

    c. A library book of each student's own choosing

    d. A short story from language arts class

4. "Language load" refers to:

    a. The basic vocabulary words a first grader has committed to memory

    b. The number of unrecognizable words an English Language Learner encounters when reading a passage or listening to a teacher

    c. The damage that carrying a pile of heavy books could cause to a child's physique

    d. The number of different languages a person has mastered.

6. According to the MLA system for documenting sources in literature, which of the following typically combines signal phrases and parenthetical references?

    a. An MLA list of the works cited

    b. MLA in-text citations in a paper

    c. Adding MLA information notes

    d. MLA footnotes

1

5. The first-grade teacher wants her class to understand that stories have a certain order. She reads them a story, then orally reviews with them how each event that happened in the story caused the next event to happen. To reinforce the lesson the teacher should:

    a. Give each child a piece of drawing paper that has been folded in half and then again, creating four boxes, along with a piece that has not been folded. The teacher should then ask the students to draw a cartoon about the story. Each of the first four boxes will show the events in order. The second page is to show how the story ends

    b. Give each child a piece of drawing paper and ask the students to draw the most important scene

    c. Give each child a piece of drawing paper and ask the students to draw the story's beginning on the front of the page and ending on the back

    d. Give each child a piece of drawing paper that has been folded in half and then again, creating four boxes, along with a piece that has not been folded. The teacher should then ask the students to draw a cartoon about anything they want. She reminds them to put their story cartoons in proper order

6. According to the MLA system for documenting sources in literature, which of the following typically combines signal phrases and parenthetical references?

    a. An MLA list of the works cited
    b. MLA in-text citations in a paper
    c. Adding MLA information notes
    d. MLA footnotes

7. Following instruction time, Ms. Pitman provides each student with a small sign that can be hung around the waist or neck. Ten children in her class receive signs displaying a single weekly vocabulary word. Five students get signs with the following: dis-; re-; pre-; un-; and mis-. The remaining students have signs with the following: -ing; -ed; -s; -less; and -ful. What is the best choice for a follow-up class activity based on this information?

    a. The students are arranged into groups to demonstrate tangibly that certain parts of the English language have fixed functions.

    b. Each student must use his or her sign to brainstorm a list of possible words that include those letters.

    c. Each time a bell is rung, students must find a new partner with whom he or she can combine signs to make a new word.

    d. Ask each student to explain what his or her sign means and how it functions in the English language.

8. At the beginning of each month, Mr. Yi has Jade read a page or two from a book she hasn't seen before. He notes the total number of words in the section, and also notes the number of times she leaves out or misreads a word. If Jade reads the passage with less than 3% error, Mr. Yi is satisfied that Jade is:

    a. Reading with full comprehension
    b. Probably bored and should try a more difficult book
    c. Reading at her Independent reading level
    d. Comfortable with the syntactical meaning

9. Which assessment will determine a student's ability to identify initial, medial, blended, final, segmented, and manipulated 'units'?

    a. Phonological awareness assessment
    b. High-frequency word assessment
    c. Reading fluency assessment
    d. Comprehension quick-check

10. When you have a writing assignment, which of the following is true about your reader audience?

    a. You need not identify the audience because it is the assigning teacher.
    b. You should consider how your readers are likely to use what you write.
    c. You should know your writing purpose more than a reader's purposes.
    d. You are overthinking to wonder about readers' likely attitude/reaction.

11. Which of the following is correct regarding phonological awareness in kindergarteners?

    a. Children with delayed language development have benefited from phonological awareness training.
    b. Researchers into instruction in phonological awareness advise against using SLPs and their methods.
    c. Phonological awareness in kindergarteners requires changing phonemes in words to change meaning.
    d. Phonological awareness instruction for kindergarteners involves only the individual phoneme level.

12. Sight words are:

    a. Common words with irregular spelling
    b. Words that can easily be found on educational websites
    c. Any word that can be seen, including text words, words on signs, brochures, banners, and so forth
    d. There is no such thing; because oral language is learned before written language, all words are ultimately based on sound. The correct term is sound words and includes all words necessary to decode a particular text

13. A second-grade teacher wants to help her students enrich their vocabulary. She's noticed that their writing journals are filled with serviceable but unexciting verbs such as "said" and "went," and general rather than specific nouns. The most effective lesson would involve:

    a. Suggesting students use a thesaurus to substitute more unusual words for common ones
    b. Suggesting students add an adjective to each noun
    c. Brainstorming a list of verbs that mean ways of talking or ways of going, then adding them to the word wall along with some nouns that specify common topics
    d. Suggesting students look up the meanings of boring words and consider another way to express them

14. Which of the following students may need extra instruction and evaluation with respect to oral language skills?

    a. Rosa: whose first language is Spanish. Rosa speaks with a distinct accent and can be difficult to understand when speaking about a new or unfamiliar topic.

    b. Greer: who avoids oral assignments when possible. He avoids speaking up in class and only responds when called upon.

    c. Ashley: who often has trouble answering questions in class. Her responses are often off-topic. She also struggles with oral presentations, seeming to present a string of unrelated facts.

    d. Brett: who frequently becomes loud and disruptive whenever group work is assigned. He often becomes involved in heated discussions with classmates when discussing ideas.

15. Which of the following factors affects ELL students' English-language literacy development?

    a. A Chinese student's L1 is not written alphabetically like English is.

    b. A Spanish student's L1 is more phonetically regular than English is.

    c. Neither one of these has any effects on L2 literacy development.

    d. Both factors affect L1 literacy development but in different ways.

16. The term "common words" means:

    a. One-syllable words with fewer than three letters. Some examples are it, an, a, I, go, to, and in. They are the first words an emergent writer learns

    b. One-syllable words with fewer than five letters. Some examples include sing, goes, sit, rock, walk, and took

    c. Words that are ordinary or unexceptional; because they tend to flatten a piece of writing, they should be avoided

    d. Familiar, frequently used words that do not need to be taught beyond primary grades

17. Which choice is <u>not</u> a cueing system used to understand unfamiliar words?

    a. Syntactic

    b. Semantic

    c. Graphophonic

    d. Auditory

18. Which of the following is most accurate regarding writing style?

    a. The kind of diction you use does not affect style.

    b. You add style later to give your writing personality.

    c. Style is unrelated to your control of your content.

    d. Your purpose for writing guides your writing style.

19. What statement is most accurate regarding the context(s) wherein students develop literacy?

    a. Students develop literacy by reading, writing, listening, and speaking.

    b. Students develop literacy by reading, writing, and listening to speech.

    c. Students develop literacy by reading and writing, not any other ways.

    d. Students develop literacy by reading as the only activity that matters.

20. The most effective strategy for decoding sight words is:

a. Segmenting sight words into syllables. Beginning readers are understandably nervous when encountering a long word that isn't familiar. Blocking off all but a single syllable at a time renders a word manageable and allows the reader a sense of control over the act of reading
b. Word families. By grouping the sight word with similar words, patterns emerge
c. A phonemic approach. When students understand the connection between individual words and their sounds, they will be able to sound out any sight word they encounter
d. None; sight words cannot be decoded. Readers must learn to recognize these words as wholes on sight

21. Editing involves:

a. Correcting surface features such as sentence fragments, spelling, and punctuation
b. Fine-tuning the underlying structure of the piece to make the theme stand out
c. Reconsidering ideas, adding or subtracting information, and changing the underlying structure
d. Adding illustrations, charts, and other useful addenda

22. A teacher wants to work on her students' listening comprehension in addition to their reading comprehension since she understands that the skills are interrelated. She has a series of short stories that she thinks the students will enjoy. Which of the following would be the best supplement to typical written comprehension exercises?

a. Preview content and then read the stories aloud to the students. Assess listening comprehension through verbal and written questions.
b. Ask the students to choose one story each to read aloud to a small group. Encourage the students to discuss what they have learned afterward.
c. Assign each student a story to read and require them to write a report on it. Each student should then present his report based on what he has learned to the class.
d. Have the students read stories aloud to the class, and create mock tests based upon the main ideas which they identify.

23. Which of the following *most* accurately summarizes the relationship of reading fluency and reading comprehension?

a. As students develop greater reading comprehension, their reading fluency also improves.
b. When students develop greater reading fluency, their reading comprehension improves.
c. The relationship between reading fluency and reading comprehension is a reciprocal one.
d. Reading fluency and reading comprehension are two separate, mainly unrelated skill sets.

24. Phonological awareness activities are:

a. Oral
b. Visual
c. Both A and B
d. Semantically based

25. William Shakespeare wrote during which historical and literary period?

a. Medieval
b. Renaissance
c. Restoration
d. Enlightenment

26. Of the following sentences, which one appeals to emotion?

    a. It is dangerous to use a cell phone while driving because you steer one-handed.
    b. Statistics of greater accident risk show cell-phone use while driving is dangerous.
    c. It is really stupid to use a cell phone when you drive because it is so dangerous.
    d. Many state laws ban cell phone use when driving due to data on more accidents.

27. To determine the subject matter of a section within a text chapter, what should the teacher tell the student to do?

    a. Read the section heading
    b. Read the chapter glossary
    c. Read the index in the text
    d. Read through the section

28. A class is reading *A Wrinkle in Time*. The teacher asks students to write a short paper explaining the story's resolution. She is asking them to locate and discuss the story's:

    a. Outcome
    b. Highest or most dramatic moment
    c. Plot
    d. Lowest point

29. In the word-recognition model of the Three Cueing Systems used in teaching reading, which of the following is most associated with the meanings of words?

    a. Using pragmatic cues
    b. Phonological system
    c. The syntactic system
    d. The semantic system

30. Abi, a fifth-grader, is reading aloud to his teacher during one-on-one reading time. His teacher uses this time to evaluate ongoing fluency and comprehension skills. Following today's reading, Abi's teacher determines that he needs practice with words that begin with digraphs. Which of the following sets of words would most likely be part of this assignment?

    a. Chicken, Shells, That
    b. Were, Frame, Click
    c. Sponge, Think, Blank
    d. Packed, Blistered, Smoothed

31. To support student vocabulary development, which of the following most accurately describes the instructional materials teachers should use?

    a. Teachers should only use literature and expository texts to support student vocabulary development.
    b. Teachers should use newspapers, magazines, etc. in addition to literature and expository textbooks.
    c. Teachers should use trade books, content-specific texts, and technology for vocabulary development.
    d. Teachers should use a broad variety of instructional materials, including all of the above and others.

32. A fifth grader has prepared a report on reptiles, which is something he knows a great deal about. He rereads his report and decides to make a number of changes. He moves a sentence from the top to the last paragraph. He crosses out several words and replaces them with more specific words. He circles key information and draws an arrow to show another place the information could logically be placed. He is engaged in:

    a. Editing
    b. Revising
    c. First editing, then revising
    d. Reviewing

33. When students are taught to use effective reading comprehension strategies, they not only achieve deeper understanding, they also learn to think about how they think when reading. This is known as...

    a. Schemata.
    b. Scaffolding.
    c. Metacognition.
    d. Metamorphosis.

34. Which exercise would be best for building fluency in young students?

    a. Allowing students to draw pictures that illustrate the texts they read if they are unable to write their responses.
    b. Using daily games and lessons to reinforce phoneme-identification skills.
    c. Placing the students into groups to read aloud to one another.
    d. Reading to the students every day from a variety of texts.

35. Which of the following correctly sequences children's typical developmental phases in writing?

    a. Beginning sounds emerge; letter-like symbols; scribbling; letter strings; initial, middle, and final sounds; consonants represent words; standard spelling; transitional phases
    b. Letter-like symbols; beginning sounds emerge; letter strings; scribbling; initial, middle, and final sounds; transitional phases; standard spelling; consonants represent words
    c. Scribbling; letter-like symbols; letter strings; beginning sounds emerge; consonants represent words; initial, middle, and final sounds; transitional phases; standard spelling
    d. Letter strings; beginning sounds emerge; initial, middle, and final sounds; consonants represent words; letter-like symbols; transitional phases; standard spelling; scribbling

36. The following is not an element of metacognition:

    a. A reader's awareness of herself as a learner
    b. A reader's understanding of a variety of reading strategies and how to apply them to comprehend a text
    c. A reader who is conscious about remembering what has been read
    d. A reader who identifies the emotions of characters in a story

37. An ESL student whose L1 is Chinese tends to omit plural endings and articles before nouns. Of the following, which is the best explanation for these errors?

    a. The student has not yet learned these English grammatical forms.
    b. Omission avoids having to choose among irregular English forms.
    c. Incompatible nature and rules of the L1 are transferring to the L2.
    d. The student does not understand how the L1 and L2 forms relate.

38. Which choice describes an appropriate alternative to Round-robin reading?

    a. All students read together, simultaneously speaking the text aloud.
    b. Students break into pairs assigned by the teacher to take turns reading the text while the teacher circulates among the pairs to guide and assess the students.
    c. The teacher reads aloud to the students before engaging in a class discussion about what they have learned.
    d. Students work on independent assignments while the teacher listens to students read individually.

39. What is the best way for teachers to help students develop larger reading and writing vocabularies?

    a. Give students weekly vocabulary lists to memorize for tests
    b. Assign students to search texts for new vocabulary words
    c. Give students many opportunities for reading and writing
    d. Assign students new-word quotas to include in writing

40. A class reads an essay about the benefits to youth of pet ownership. The author's position is very clear: She believes young people should be given the responsibility of taking care of pets. The author cites facts, research studies, and statistics to strengthen her position. This type of writing is called:

    a. Expository
    b. Narrative
    c. Persuasive
    d. Didactic

41. We are familiar with the modern English meanings of the word "disaster." But in the 16th century, this word meant...

    a. Catastrophe.
    b. Star-crossed.
    c. A misfortune.
    d. Unflowerlike.

42. Amelia has been having trouble in her 1st-grade class for several months. When her teacher, Mrs. Gant, calls Amelia for one-on-one reading practice, Amelia avoids her and protests that she is working on something else at the time. Amelia knows all her letter-sounds when she sees them individually. However, she still cannot consistently decode simple words. Amelia often seems "lost" when her teacher gives her instructions or explains an activity to the group. She usually needs to ask several times for directions to be repeated and oftentimes does not understand what is being asked of her. Amelia sometimes misbehaves in class, hiding during lesson time or arguing with other students during group activities. Which language disorder most closely matches Amelia's symptoms?

    a. Anomic aphasia
    b. Auditory processing disorder
    c. Dysgraphia
    d. Dyslexia

43. Among these forms of electronic media, which have the highest level of formality?

    a. Web news articles
    b. Blogs on the web
    c. Email messages
    d. All are the same

44. An ORF is:

    a. An Oral Reading Fluency assessment
    b. An Occasional Reading Function assessment
    c. An Oscar Reynolds Feinstein assessment
    d. An Overt Reading Failure assessment

45. Which of the following is NOT typically categorized as a prewriting process?

    a. Planning
    b. Reflection
    c. Visualization
    d. Brainstorming

46. Activating prior knowledge, shared reading, and using graphic organizers are all examples of what type of instructional concept?

    a. Modeling
    b. Scaffolding
    c. Assessing
    d. Inspiring

47. Which of the following is not true regarding grammar instruction?

    a. Grammar is primarily important in writing; therefore, it must be taught predominantly within the context of writing instruction.
    b. Teachers must not only teach grammatical concepts in abstract, but also show students how to contextualize that knowledge and apply it to reading, writing, and speaking.
    c. Knowledge of grammar can be both declarative and procedural in nature.
    d. Many students find grammar to be "boring," necessitating engaging teaching methods and discussions about why grammatical knowledge is important.

48. The ratio of employee wages and benefits to all other operational costs of a business is 2:3. If a business's total operating expenses are $130,000 per month, how much money does the company spend on employee wages and benefits?

    a. $43,333.33
    b. $86,666.67
    c. $52,000.00
    d. $78,000.00

49. Given that x is a prime number and that the greatest common factor of x and y is greater than 1, compare the two quantities.

Quantity A	Quantity B
y	the least common multiple of x and y

    a. Quantity A is greater.
    b. Quantity B is greater.
    c. The two quantities are the same.
    d. The relationship cannot be determined from the given information.

50. If 1" on a map represents 60 ft, how many yards apart are two points if the distance between the points on the map is 10"?

    a. 1800
    b. 600
    c. 200
    d. 2

51. The vertices of a polygon are $(2,3)$, $(8,1)$, $(6, -5)$, and $(0, -3)$. Which of the following describes the polygon most specifically?

    a. Parallelogram
    b. Rhombus
    c. Rectangle
    d. Square

52. Which of these tables properly displays the measures of central tendency which can be used for nominal, interval, and ordinal data?

a.

	Mean	Median	Mode
Nominal			x
Interval	x	x	x
Ordinal		x	x

b.

	Mean	Median	Mode
Nominal			x
Interval	x	x	x
Ordinal	x	x	x

c.

	Mean	Median	Mode
Nominal	x	x	x
Interval	x	x	x
Ordinal	x	x	x

d.

	Mean	Median	Mode
Nominal			x
Interval	x	x	
Ordinal	x	x	x

The box-and-whisker plot displays student test scores by class period. Use the data to answer questions 53 through 54:

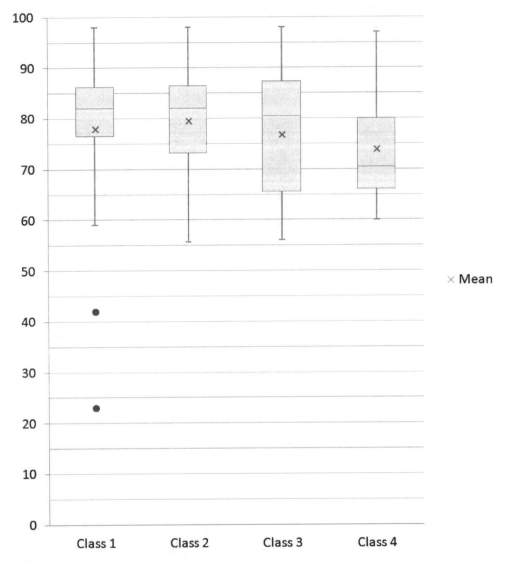

53. Which class has the greatest range of test scores?
    a. Class 1
    b. Class 2
    c. Class 3
    d. Class 4

54. What is the probability that a student chosen at random from class 2 made above a 73 on this test?
    a. 0.25
    b. 0.5
    c. 0.6
    d. 0.75

55. A random sample of students at an elementary school were asked these three questions:

    Do you like carrots?
    Do you like broccoli?
    Do you like cauliflower?

The results of the survey are shown below. If these data are representative of the population of students at the school, which of these is most probable?

    a. A student chosen at random likes broccoli.
    b. If a student chosen at random likes carrots, he also likes at least one other vegetable.
    c. If a student chosen at random likes cauliflower and broccoli, he also likes carrots.
    d. A student chosen at random does not like carrots, broccoli, or cauliflower.

56. Robert buys a car for $24,210. The price of the car has been marked down by 10%. What was the original price of the car?

    a. $25,900
    b. $26,300
    c. $26,900
    d. $27,300

57. Which of the following formulas may be used to represent the sequence 8, 13, 18, 23, 28, ...?

    a. $a_n = 5n + 3$
    b. $a_n = n + 5$
    c. $a_n = n + 8$
    d. $a_n = 5n + 8$

58. Elijah pays a $30 park entrance fee, plus $4 for every ticket purchased. Which of the following equations represents the cost?

    a. y = 30x + 4
    b. y = 34x
    c. y = 4x + 30
    d. y = 34x + 30

59. Hannah spends at least $16 on 4 packages of coffee. Which of the following inequalities represents the possible costs?

    a. 16 ≥ 4p
    b. 16 < 4p
    c. 16 > 4p
    d. 16 ≤ 4p

60. A cylindrical carrot stick is sliced with a knife. Which of the following shapes is *not* a possible cross-section?

    a. circle
    b. rectangle
    c. ellipse
    d. triangle

61. Adam rolls a standard six-sided die. What is the probability he rolls a number greater than or equal to 5?

    a. $\frac{1}{6}$

    b. $\frac{1}{5}$

    c. $\frac{1}{4}$

    d. $\frac{1}{3}$

62. A teacher is working with her students on a unit on subtraction. She notices that most students are much more successful when working the problems with manipulatives rather than working the problems with numerals. In which stage of development are most of her students operating?

    a. Formal operations stage
    b. Concrete operations stage
    c. Pre-operations stage
    d. Sensory motor stage

63. During February, the sixth-grade teachers at an elementary school decide to work together to teach a unit about the heart. The English teacher will have the students write essays about how the heart functions. The science teacher will teach the basic parts of the heart. The art teacher will have the students build models of the heart. The math teacher will have the students determine the amount of blood that flows through the heart in everyday units of capacity.

The teachers are implementing the concept of which of the following?

    a. Differentiated instruction
    b. Formative assessment
    c. Thematic units
    d. Collaborative learning

64. Which of the following correctly compares the given rational numbers?

    a. $0.2 > 0.0499 > 0.007$
    b. $0 < -2 < 7$
    c. $\frac{1}{5} > \frac{1}{4} > \frac{1}{3}$
    d. $-1 < -4 < -10$

65. A jogger records his distance in meters from his front door as a function of time in seconds on his morning run. If x represents time in seconds, which of the following equations represents the jogger's distance from his front door as a function of time?

Time	0	3	4	6	7
Distance	5.2	25.0	31.6	44.8	51.4

    a. $y = 3x + 25$
    b. $y = 25.0x + 5.2$
    c. $y = 18.4x + 3$
    d. $y = 6.6x + 5.2$

66. Which of the following equations is a linear equation?

a. $y = x^2 + 4$
b. $y = \frac{2}{x^3}$
c. $2x - 3y = 5$
d. $x = (y + 2)^2$

67. Which of the following correctly explains one method that may be used to determine the size of each angle in a regular polygon of more than four sides?

a. Draw all possible diagonals of the polygon. The sum of the angles of the polygon is equal to the product of the number of triangles formed and 180°. Finally, divide this sum by the number of sides of the polygon.
b. Choose one vertex of the polygon and draw diagonals from that vertex to all nonconsecutive vertices. The sum of the angles of the polygon is equal to the area of the triangles formed. Finally, divide the sum by the number of triangles formed.
c. Draw all possible diagonals of the polygon. The sum of the angles of the polygon is equal to the product of the number of triangles formed and 180°. Finally, divide the sum by the number of triangles formed.
d. Choose one vertex of the polygon and draw diagonals from that vertex to all nonconsecutive vertices. The sum of the angles of the polygon is equal to the product of the number of triangles formed and 180°. Finally, divide this sum by the number of sides of the polygon.

68. Mr. Gomez is a sixth-grade teacher presenting a unit on compound probability. He places ten marbles with the digits 0 through 9 in a bowl on his podium. He draws a marble, records the number, and then places the marble back in the bowl. He repeats the process. What is the probability that he drew two 5s in a row?

a. 1/10
b. 1/5
c. 1/100
d. 1/50

69. Mr. Carver is teaching his students about deductive reasoning and states the premises listed below. Which of these students has reached a valid conclusion?

| Premise 1 | All primates are mammals. |
| Premise 2 | All lemurs are primates. |

a. Mia states, "All primates are lemurs."
b. Carlos states, "All lemurs are mammals."
c. Xavier states, "All whales are mammals."
d. Gavin states, "All monkeys are primates."

70. Which of the following accurately describes the set of integers?

a. the set of counting numbers
b. the set of counting numbers, plus zero
c. the set of numbers that may be written as the ratio of $\frac{a}{b}$, where $b \neq 0$
d. the set of counting numbers, zero, and the negations of the counting numbers

71. Jackson can decorate a cake in 3 hours. Eli can decorate the same cake in 2 hours. If they work together, how long will it take them to decorate the cake?

    a. 0.8 hours
    b. 1.2 hours
    c. 1.5 hours
    d. 1.8 hours

72. Given that the two horizontal lines in the diagram below are parallel, which of the following statements is correct?

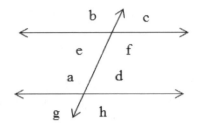

    a. Angles b and g are complementary.
    b. Angles d and c are supplementary.
    c. Angles a and e are supplementary.
    d. Angles e and h are congruent.

73. What scale factor was applied to the larger triangle to obtain the smaller triangle below?

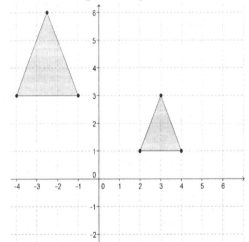

    a. $\frac{1}{4}$
    b. $\frac{1}{3}$
    c. $\frac{1}{2}$
    d. $\frac{2}{3}$

74. Given the boxplots below, which of the following statements is correct?

a. Data Set A has a larger range and a larger median.
b. Data Set A has a smaller range and a larger median.
c. Data Set A has a larger range and a smaller median.
d. Data Set A has a smaller range and a smaller median.

75. A sheriff's office in a small town creates a chart of violent crimes in the area for the year of 2005. Based on the chart below, which prediction for 2006 seems the most appropriate?

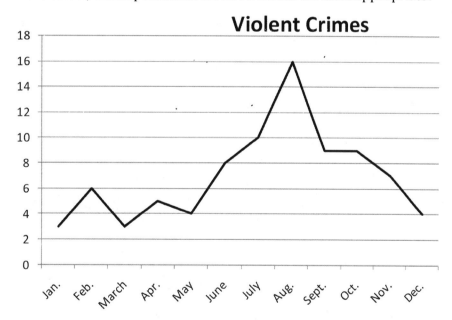

a. The winter months are likely to see a spike in violent crime rates.
b. Holiday months will likely see an increase in personal theft.
c. Violent crimes will be greatest when the weather is the warmest.
d. The number of violent crimes per month will continue to grow throughout the year.

76. In a town of 35,638 people, about a quarter of the population is under the age of 35. Of those, just over a third attend local K-12 schools. If the number of students in each grade is about the same, how many fourth graders likely reside in the town?

    a. Fewer than 100
    b. Between 200 and 300
    c. Between 300 and 400
    d. More than 400

77. To which of the following sets of numbers does -4 **NOT** belong?

    a. The set of whole numbers
    b. The set of rational numbers
    c. The set of integers
    d. The set of real numbers

78. Which of these does **NOT** have a solution set of $\{x: -1 \leq x \leq 1\}$?

    a. $-4 \leq 2 + 3(x - 1) \leq 2$
    b. $-2x^2 + 2 \geq x^2 - 1$
    c. $\frac{11 - |3x|}{7} \geq 2$
    d. $3|2x| + 4 \leq 10$

79. A triangle with vertices $A(-4,2)$, $B(-1,3)$, and $C(-5,7)$ is reflected across $y = x + 2$ to give $\Delta A'B'C'$, which is subsequently reflected across the y-axis to give $\Delta A''B''C''$. Which of these statements is true?

    a. A 90° rotation of ΔABC about $(-2,0)$ gives $\Delta A''B''C''$.
    b. A reflection of ΔABC about the x-axis gives $\Delta A''B''C''$.
    c. A 270° rotation of ΔABC about $(0,2)$ gives $\Delta A''B''C''$.
    d. A translation of ΔABC two units down gives $\Delta A''B''C''$.

Use the following data to answer questions 80-82:

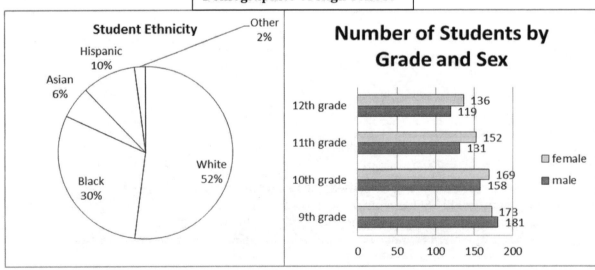

80. Which of these is the greatest quantity?

    a. The average number of male students in the 11th and 12th grades
    b. The number of Hispanic students at the school
    c. The difference in the number of male and female students at the school
    d. The difference in the number of 9th and 12th grade students at the school

81. Compare the two quantities.

Quantity A	Quantity B
The percentage of white students at the school, rounded to the nearest whole number 633	The percentage of female students at the school, rounded to the nearest whole number 630

    a. Quantity A is greater.
    b. Quantity B is greater.
    c. The two quantities are the same.
    d. The relationship cannot be determined from the given information.

82. An eleventh grader is chosen at random to represent the school at a conference. What is the approximate probability that the student is male?

    a. 0.03
    b. 0.11
    c. 0.22
    d. 0.46

83. Attending a summer camp are 12 six-year-olds, 15 seven-year-olds, 14 eight-year-olds, 12 nine-year-olds, and 10 ten-year-olds. If a camper is randomly selected to participate in a special event, what is the probability that he or she is at least eight years old?

    a. $\frac{2}{9}$
    b. $\frac{22}{63}$
    c. $\frac{4}{7}$
    d. $\frac{3}{7}$

84. Carlos spends $\frac{1}{8}$ of his monthly salary on utility bills. If his utility bills total $320, what is his monthly salary?

    a. $2,440
    b. $2,520
    c. $2,560
    d. $2,600

85. Which of the following empire(s) no longer existed following the armistice ending World War I?

    a. The Austro-Hungarian Empire
    b. The Ottoman Empire
    c. The German Empire
    d. All of these empires

86. What is the main difference between a primary election and a caucus?

   a. A primary election is privately run by political parties, and a caucus is held by local governments
   b. Caucuses are always held on the same day, but the dates of state primaries vary
   c. A caucus is privately run by political parties, and a primary is an indirect election run by state and local governments
   d. Primary elections are all held on the same date, but the dates of caucuses vary

87. How are members of the Federal Judiciary chosen?

   a. They are elected by voters
   b. They are appointed by the President and confirmed by the House of Representatives
   c. They are chosen by a committee
   d. They are appointed by the President and confirmed by the Senate

88. Which of the following conquistadores unwittingly gave smallpox to the Indians and destroyed the Aztec empire in Mexico?

   a. Balboa
   b. Ponce de Leon
   c. Cortes
   d. De Vaca

89. Which of the following statements is true regarding the Puritans?

   a. In terms of their theology, the Puritans were considered Calvinists
   b. Many Puritans agreed with the radical criticisms of the Swiss Calvinists
   c. Many of those identified as Calvinists opposed the Puritans
   d. All these statements are true regarding the Puritan movement

90. An economist who advocated government intervention to prevent and remedy recessions and depressions was:

   a. Adam Smith.
   b. John Maynard Keynes.
   c. Friedrich Hayek.
   d. Milton Friedman.

91. The Supreme Court has nine members. How is this number determined?

   a. It is outlined in the Constitution
   b. Congress determines the number
   c. The President determines the number
   d. The Court decides on the number

92. The first amendment guarantees all below except:

   a. Freedom of assembly
   b. The right to bear arms
   c. Freedom of the press
   d. The right to speak freely

93. Which of the following is *not* one of the core demographic variables?

    a. Fertility
    b. Diversity
    c. Mortality
    d. Migration

94. John Maynard Keynes advocated what?

    a. Supply-side economics
    b. Demand-side economics
    c. Laissez-faire economics
    d. The Laffer Curve

95. The bubonic plague spread through Europe in which of the following ways?

    a. It spread along rivers and through contaminated drinking water
    b. It was carried by birds that migrated south during the winter
    c. It spread along trade routes, carried by infected animals and people on ships
    d It was carried by travelers on religious pilgrimages

96. Which of the following was *not* an immediate effect of rapid urban growth in the 1800s?

    a. Poor sanitation conditions in the cities
    b. Epidemics of diseases in the cities
    c. Inadequate police and fire protection
    d. Widespread urban political corruption

97. Which of the following is the best example of a factor resulting from Europe's Commercial Revolution that contributed to the 1700s' Industrial Revolution?

    a. The rediscovery of concrete
    b. New advances in making iron
    c. The steam engine's invention
    d. Increases in population growth

98. A group that grew in numbers as a result of the Industrial Revolution was:

    a. Small farmers.
    b. Unskilled workers.
    c. Skilled craftsmen.
    d. The rural population.

99. The primary expense for most state and local governments is:

    a. Emergency medical services
    b. Transportation services
    c. Police and fire departments
    d. Education

100. Of the following, which person or group was *not* instrumental in the advancement of civil rights and desegregation during the 1940s and 1950s?

    a. The President
    b. The Supreme Court
    c. The Congress
    d. The NAACP

101. Which of the following is true of social changes and the Industrial Revolution in Europe in the 18th and early 19th centuries?

    a. They gave rise to a new middle-class
    b. They improved working conditions
    c. They were the result of urbanization
    d. They were caused by the labor unions

102. Which Supreme Court case enforced the civil rights of citizens to not incriminate themselves?

    a. Marbury v. Madison
    b. Miranda v. Arizona
    c. Youngstown Sheet and Tube Company v. Sawyer
    d. United States v. Carolene Products Company

103. Which of the following are true of the demand curve?

    I. It is normally downward sloping
    II. It is normally upward sloping
    III. It is influenced by the law of diminishing marginal unity
    IV. It is unaffected by the law of diminishing marginal unity

    a. I and III only
    b. I and IV only
    c. II and III only
    d. II and IV only

104. The economy of colonial New England focused on manufacture and trade mainly because:

    a. soil and climate conditions in New England were not conducive to year-round farming.
    b. the New England colonists were primarily merchants from England and Scotland.
    c. slavery did not exist in the northern colonies.
    d. the New England colonists wanted to achieve economic dominance over the Middle Atlantic colonies.

105. Which of the following world religions believes in many gods and goddesses?

    a. Confucianism
    b. Hinduism
    c. Sikhism
    d. Islam

106. The President serves as Commander-in-Chief. What are the President's two limitations in that role?

    a. The President cannot declare war or oversee military regulations
    b. The President cannot enforce blockades or declare war
    c. The President cannot enforce quarantines or oversee military regulations
    d. The President cannot enforce blockades or quarantines

107. When the prices farmers receive for their crops decline in a developing country, this typically results in which of the following?

    a. Increased urbanization
    b. Increased college enrollment
    c. Declining literacy rates
    d. Higher prices for those crops in developed countries

108. Which of the following is *not* true about the Crusades?

    a. Their purpose was for European rulers to retake the Middle East from Muslims
    b. The Crusades succeeded at European kings' goal of reclaiming the "holy land"
    c. The Crusades accelerated the already incipient decline of the Byzantine Empire
    d. Egypt saw a return as a major Middle Eastern power as a result of the Crusades

109. Every citizen 18 years of age and older has the constitutional right to vote. What do states govern in the voting process?

    a. The registration for elections
    b. The administration of elections
    c. Both A and B
    d. State governments are not involved in federal elections

110. Who may write a bill?

    a. Anyone
    b. A member of the House
    c. A Senator
    d. Any member of Congress

111. Which biome features scrubby plants and small evergreen trees and also has a hot, dry summer followed by a wetter winter?

    a. Taiga
    b. Coniferous forest
    c. Chaparral
    d. Savanna

112. Which of these was NOT an immediate consequence of the Age of Exploration?

    a. the development of more accurate navigation instruments
    b. the introduction of new foods and other goods to Europe
    c. the decline of England as a world power
    d. the discovery of new lands where people might seek a better life

113. What causes the motion of glaciers?

    a. Gravity
    b. Erosion
    c. Wind
    d. Temperature change

114. What term is used to describe two waves that are out of phase as they come together to produce a new wave?

    a. Incomplete interference
    b. Distorted interference
    c. Constructive interference
    d. Destructive interference

115. What part of a plant system responds to stimuli by releasing water via transpiration, except during adverse conditions like a drought when it closes up to prevent the plant from dehydration?

    a. Pith
    b. Stomata
    c. Guard cells
    d. Sepals

116. The boiling of water is an example of ____:

    a. a physical change.
    b. a chemical change.
    c. sublimation.
    d. condensation.

117. When using a light microscope, how is the total magnification determined?

    a. By multiplying the ocular lens power times the objective being used.
    b. By looking at the objective you are using only.
    c. By looking at the ocular lens power only.
    d. By multiplying the objective you are using times two.

118. Why do balloons filled with helium float while balloons filled with air do not float?

    a. Balloons filled with air are larger than balloons filled with helium, which makes them heavier preventing them from floating
    b. Helium is less dense than air, which allows balloons filled with helium to float
    c. Helium balloons travel on higher air currents and balloons filled with air travel on lower air currents
    d. Air causes balloons to generate static electricity so the balloon will be attracted to the ground

119. Which of the following sources of fresh water is unavailable for human use?

    a. Rivers
    b. Estuaries
    c. Aquifers
    d. Glaciers

120. When heat is removed from water during condensation, new ____ form.

    a. atoms
    b. covalent bonds
    c. intermolecular bonds
    d. ionic bonds

121. The amount of potential energy an object has depends on all of the following except its

    a. mass.
    b. height above ground.
    c. gravitational attraction.
    d. temperature.

122. Which statement accurately describes a state of matter?

    a. Solids take the shape of their container
    b. Gasses maintain a fixed shape
    c. Liquids will expand to fill the volume of a container
    d. Gasses expand to fill an entire space

123. Which of the following situations would result in the generation of new crust?

    a. Two crustal plates converge.
    b. Two crustal plates move apart.
    c. Two crustal plates slide past one another.
    d. A crustal plate is pushed down into the mantle.

124. What is the purpose of conducting an experiment?

    a. to test a hypothesis
    b. to collect data
    c. to identify a control state
    d. to choose variables

125. A long nail is heated at one end. After a few seconds, the other end of the nail becomes equally hot. What type of heat transfer does this represent?

    a. Radiation
    b. Conduction
    c. Convection
    d. Entropy

126. Which of the following would increase the reaction rate of a chemical reaction?

    a. Low kinetic energy
    b. Low-temperature
    c. High concentration
    d. High activation energy

127. Which of the following is an example of a trace fossil?

    a. A mouse jaw
    b. A footprint
    c. A shark tooth
    d. A cast of a skull

128. When two tectonic plates are moving laterally in opposing directions, this is called a:

    a. Transform boundary.
    b. Compressional boundary.
    c. Oppositional boundary.
    d. Lateral boundary.

129. If an atom's outer shell is filled, what must be true?

    a. It reacts with other atoms through chemical reactions.
    b. It exchanges electrons to form bonds with other atoms.
    c. It has 32 electrons in its outer shell.
    d. It is a stable atom.

130. What type of substance is least likely to be soluble in water?

    a. Ionic
    b. Polar
    c. Hydrophilic
    d. Non-polar

131. Which of the following describes the physical or non-biological part of the carbon cycle?

    a. Phytoplankton use carbon dioxide and other nutrients to produce carbohydrates and oxygen.
    b. Cold water dissolves atmospheric carbon dioxide, stores it, and releases it back out to the atmosphere as needed.
    c. Carbon dioxide is dissolved in sea water and is broken up to free carbon for use by marine life.
    d. Warm, surface water dissolves carbon dioxide where it is converted to nitrogen and phosphorus for use by marine life.

132. In a food chain, where does energy go after the secondary consumer dies?

    a. Back to the Sun
    b. To the producers
    c. Into the air, becomes wind
    d. To decomposers

133. When you walk barefoot on a hot sidewalk, what process is primarily responsible for heat transfer from the sidewalk to your foot?

    a. Conduction
    b. Convection
    c. Radiation
    d. None of the above.

134. Where is the type of RNA that carries and positions amino acids for further assembly located in the cell?

    a. Cytoplasm
    b. Nucleus
    c. Ribosome
    d. Mitochondria

135. What other planet in the solar system experiences a greenhouse effect similar to that observed on Earth?

    a. Mercury
    b. Venus
    c. Neptune
    d. Saturn

136. The energy radiated by stars is produced by:

    a. Neutronicity.
    b. Nuclear fusion.
    c. Nuclear fission.
    d. Gravitational confinement.

137. If a glass rod is rubbed with a cloth made of polyester, what will the resulting charge be on each material?

a. The charge on the glass rod is positive and the charge on the cloth is negative.
b. The charge on the glass rod is negative and the charge on the cloth is positive.
c. The charge on the glass rod is neutral and the charge on the cloth is positive.
d. The charge on the glass rod and the cloth both become neutral.

138. What do all animals belonging to the Echinodermata phylum have in common?

a. They use multiple appendages for locomotion.
b. They use tube feet for locomotion and feeding.
c. They have an exoskeleton made of chitin.
d. They must shed their outer layer of skin to grow.

139. Which of the following creates an electromagnet?

a. alignment of protons inside a metal conductor
b. an iron bar moving inside a coil of wire that contains a current
c. the movement of electrons through a complete circuit
d. convection currents within the liquid core of Earth's interior

140. Which of the following is a proposed explanation for the formation of black holes?

a. High-energy collisions
b. Gravitational collapse
c. Accretion of matter
d. A and B

Answer Key and Explanations

1. A: Proficiency with oral language enhances students' phonemic awareness and increases vocabulary. Understanding that words are scripted with specific letters representing specific sounds is essential to decoding a text. Students cannot effectively learn to read without the ability to decode. An enhanced vocabulary supports the act of reading; the larger an emergent reader's vocabulary, the more quickly he will learn to read. He will be able to decode more words, which he can organize into word families, which he can use to decode unfamiliar words.

2. D: This description is most typical of the process of peer review. Classmates read Arthur's paper and then they identify values in it, describe it, ask questions about it, and suggest points for revision. These are types of helpful feedback identified by experts on writing and collaborative writing. The other choices, however, are not typically collaborative. For a portfolio assessment (A), the teacher collects finished work products from a student over time, eventually assembling a portfolio of work. This affords a more authentic assessment using richer, more multidimensional, and more visual and tactile products for assessment instead of using only standardized test scores for assessment. Holistic scoring (B) is a method of scoring a piece of writing for overall quality (evaluating general elements such as focus, organization, support, and conventions) rather than being overly concerned with any individual aspect of writing. A scoring rubric (C) is a guide that gives examples of the levels of typical characteristics in a piece of writing that correspond to each available score (for example, scores from 1-5).

3. B: Previewing and reviewing are skills that assist in learning detailed or large amounts of information. Using these concepts, students learn skills such as skimming and outlining to get an idea of what the text is about before actually reading it. After reading, the students learn to review the information they learned and compare it to their initial previews. This method is particularly helpful when individuals are reading in order to learn new information, as they would be when reading their science texts.

4. B: The number of unrecognizable words an English Language Learner encounters when reading a passage or listening to a teacher. Language load is one of the barriers English Language Learners face. To lighten this load, a teacher can rephrase, eliminate unnecessary words, divide complex sentences into smaller units, and teach essential vocabulary before the student begins the lesson.

5. B: The MLA (Modern Language Association) system for documenting literary sources defines in-line citations in a paper as combining signal phrases, which usually include the author name and introduce information from a source via a fact, summary, paraphrase, or quotation; parenthetical references following the material cited, frequently at the end of the sentence; and, except for web sources that are unpaginated, page number(s). MLA defines a list of works cited (A) as an alphabetized list found at the end of a research paper that gives the information sources referenced in the paper, including each source's publication information, quotations, summaries, and paraphrases. Guidelines for preparing the list of works cited are provided in the *MLA Handbook*. MLA information notes (C) are an optional addition to the MLA parenthetical documentation system. These notes can be used to add important material without interrupting the paper's flow, and/or to supply comments about sources or make references to multiple sources. They may be endnotes or footnotes. Thus, choice D is also incorrect.

6. A: Give each child a piece of drawing paper that has been folded in half and then again, creating four boxes, along with a piece that has not been folded. The teacher should then ask the students to draw a cartoon about the story. Each of the first four boxes will show the events in order. The second page is to show how the story ends. When a child is able to visually see the way a familiar story has unfolded, that child can find causal or thematic connections in the action that increases her comprehension of the story overall. Asking the class to draw a single picture or to draw the beginning and end doesn't sufficiently demonstrate the importance of order to meaning. While some first graders may be able to create their own cartoon stories that demonstrate a logical series of events, many first graders are not yet ready to organize thought into a linear progression.

7. C: One-half of the class receives signs showing vocabulary words, which are probably used as root words. Remaining students are split into two general groups: those with prefixes on their signs and those with suffixes. The best approach is to get the students moving, listening, and talking in order to solidify their understanding of how roots, suffixes, and prefixes work together to make new meanings out of various root words. This approach also allows the students to participate in a game in a group context, making the activity more fun and engaging.

8. C: Reading at her Independent reading level. When reading independently, students are at the correct level if they read with at least 97% accuracy.

9. A: The words in this question prompt are most often used to refer to *sounds* made while reading. Initial/onset, medial, and final sounds are decoded in the beginning, middle, and end of words. When a teacher needs to assess an emergent or struggling reader's ability to differentiate between sounds in words, he or she may use a phonological awareness assessment. This tool will provide the teacher with information about the student's current ability to decode or encode words.

10. B: For any writing assignment, you should first target an audience, perform an audience analysis, and develop an audience profile to determine what you should include in and omit from your writing. Even though the assigning teacher may be the only one to read your writing, you should not assume s/he is your main audience (A) because the teacher may expect you to write for other readers. In addition to first knowing your purpose for writing before beginning, you should also consider what purpose your writing will meet for your readers (C) and how they are likely to use it. Considering what your audience's attitudes toward what you will write and their likely reactions to it is also important to shaping your writing and is NOT overthinking (D).

11. A: Multiple research studies have found that teaching phonological awareness skills to kindergartners with delayed language development has enhanced their language development. Researchers also recommend involving speech-language pathologists (SLPs) and their instructional methods as effective in teaching phonological awareness skills (B). Phonological awareness involves being able to recognize and change phonemes (speech sounds) without any reference to meanings (C) of words, syllables, or morphological units. Researchers and others instructing kindergartners in phonological awareness skills have provided training at both the individual phoneme level (identifying and differentiating phonemes, matching initial and final phonemes, deleting phonemes, blending phonemes, etc.) and above (D) the phoneme level (syllable, word, and rhyme awareness).

12. A: Common words with irregular spelling. Sight words occur in many types of writing; they are high-frequency words. Sight words are also words with irregular spelling. Some examples of sight words include *talk, some,* and *the.* Fluent readers need to recognize these words visually.

13. C: Brainstorming a list of verbs that mean ways of talking or ways of going, then adding them to the word wall along with some nouns that specify common topics. Second graders aren't developmentally ready for a thesaurus; most will believe that any words in a particular list are interchangeable. For example, a student who wrote *my little sister walks like a baby* might find the verbs *strut, sidle,* and *amble* in the thesaurus. None of these verbs would be an appropriate substitution. Supplementing a noun with an adjective often results in flat writing: *There's a tree in my yard* might become *There's a nice tree in my big yard.* Adjectives such as *pretty, fun, cute, funny,* and so forth don't add much in terms of meaning, but they are the adjectives younger writers reach for first. A more specific noun is both more meaningful and more interesting. *There's a weeping willow in my yard* is evocative.

14. C: Oral language skills can be distinguished from specific speech characteristics exhibited by some children. Many students like Rosa, whose first language is not English, will speak with an accent and may be less clear when speaking about a topic that is unfamiliar. In fact, even those who are not English Language Learners may exhibit difficulty speaking on new topics. Greer may avoid oral assignments or speaking in class for a number of reasons, such as self-consciousness. This student could be helped by evaluating oral language skills in a one-on-one environment or by introducing peer scaffolding to help reduce anxiety. Brett's demeanor in group assignments may also be due to social characteristics rather than oral skills; it would be important to evaluate his skills in various contexts. Ashley, however, shows marked problems communicating orally both in class discussion and in prepared assignments. She would benefit from specific instruction related to presenting ideas orally.

15. D: The Chinese written language is ideographic rather than alphabetic (A)—i.e., its written symbols represent concepts visually rather than being letters representing speech sounds. Also, the fact that Spanish is much more phonetically regular than English (B)—i.e., many more words are pronounced the same way as they are spelled than in English—contribute different effects to ELL students' English-language literacy development. Therefore, choice C is incorrect.

16. D: Familiar, frequently used words that do not need to be taught beyond primary grades. Common or basic words are the first tier of three-tier words. These words are widely used across the spoken and written spectrum. Some examples are *walk, go, wish, the, look, happy,* and *always.* This essential vocabulary is taught early in a reader's instruction, and beyond that it need not be taught.

17. D: There are various cueing systems that readers can use to help them understand how to read or comprehend unfamiliar words. Semantic cueing helps with understanding word meaning; the reader uses the meaning of the words around an unfamiliar word to understand what that word means. Syntactical cueing can also be called "grammatical cueing," in which a reader uses the syntax of a sentence to understand more about an unfamiliar word. Graphophonic cueing is most useful in decoding, or breaking words down into smaller components new words.

18. D: Knowing your purpose for writing means knowing what you want to achieve with the content of your writing, and knowing this will determine your writing style. Your choice of words and how formal or informal your writing is—your diction—*does* affect your style (A). Diction and tone should be consistent in your writing style, and should reflect vocabulary and writing patterns that suit your writing purpose best. Style is not added later to give writing personality (B). It develops from your purpose for writing, or what you want to accomplish with your writing. Style *is* directly related to your control of the content (C) of your writing.

19. A: Students develop literacy within multiple contexts by learning to listen to, speak, read, and write language. Therefore, it is inaccurate to say that only reading, writing, and listening (B) are activities for developing literacy. Literacy development is not confined to reading and writing (C) as some non-educators may believe. Some may even have the mistaken impression that reading is the only activity important for literacy development (D). However, literacy develops through all activities using language.

20. D: None; sight words cannot be decoded. Readers must learn to recognize these words as wholes on sight. Sight words have irregular spelling. Segmenting them into syllables or using a phonemic approach are ineffective strategies to aid a reader in recognizing a sight word because these approaches depend on rules a sight word doesn't follow. Word families group words that share common patterns of consonants and vowels. The spelling of those words is, therefore, regular because they follow a predictable pattern. Sight words are irregular and do not follow a predictable pattern and must be instantaneously recognized for writing fluency. No decoding is useful.

21. A: Correcting surface features such as sentence fragments, spelling, and punctuation. Editing is the final step in the writing process. The writer has already decided the ideas or events are in proper order, have been sufficiently described, and are clear. Now the writer turns her attention to surface features, "scrubbing" errors in spelling, punctuation, and syntax from the writing.

22. A: In choice A, the teacher guides previewing of information to show students how to put themselves in the right frame of mind to listen carefully for meaning. Students are then able to listen in a guided way based upon the previewing. By varying the type of comprehension assessment, the teacher will get a better understanding of what the students learned. Choice B is a good exercise, but does not provide for direct instruction by the teacher or a particularly skilled student. In Choice C, students are focusing more on reading comprehension than listening since they must read the story to themselves and then write a report. There is then no way to gauge what they have learned. Choice D would be useful, but does not include teacher-guided previewing, which is very helpful in building comprehension.

23. C: Researchers and educators have found that reading fluency and reading comprehension are closely linked: the more fluently a student can read, the more able the student's brain is to process the meaning of text. For example, developing automaticity of word identification enhances comprehension. Conversely, the better a student can understand the text, the more fluently s/he can read it. Therefore, while choices A and B are both true, each represents only half of the relationship whereas choice C indicates the relationship's mutual nature; and choice D is incorrect as reading fluency and reading comprehension are interrelated components in deriving meaning from text and not separate.

24. A: Oral. Phonological awareness refers to an understanding of the sounds a word makes. While phonological awareness leads to fluent reading skills, activities designed to develop an awareness of word sounds are, by definition, oral.

25. B: Shakespeare (1564-1616) wrote during the Renaissance. The Medieval (A) era (also known as the Middle Ages) was earlier, ending before the 16th century (circa 1485), and included authors like Geoffrey Chaucer, Dante Alighieri, the Pearl Poet and author of *Sir Gawain and the Green Knight,* and Sir Thomas Malory. The Restoration (C) period followed the Renaissance, circa 1660-1700, and included authors like John Dryden, who wrote poetry, satire, and criticism. The Enlightenment (D) occurred from 1700-1785 and included the authors Jonathan Swift, Alexander Pope, Dr. Samuel Johnson and James Boswell.

26. C: This sentence appeals to the reader's emotions by stating simply that it is dangerous and "really stupid" to use a cell phone while driving; it does not provide any evidence or logic to support the statement. Choice A offers a logical, common-sense argument in that steering one-handed makes driving more dangerous. Choice B refers to statistics of greater accident risk to support the statement that cell phone use while driving is dangerous. Such supporting evidence is an appeal to logic. Choice D cites the fact that many state laws ban cell phone use while driving to support the idea that it is dangerous, and also refers to data on more accidents from doing so. These pieces of supporting evidence also appeal to logic rather than emotion.

27. A: Students need to know why and how to use text features to inform their reading. Reading headings above sections within chapters (A) help students determine the main subject matter of each section. Reading the glossary for a chapter (B) gives students definitions of terms used in the chapter. Reading the index in a text (C) is a way to locate page numbers of references to subjects or authors in the text. Whether they will be reading the entire section or not, students need not read through the whole thing (D) only to determine its subject matter when its heading will typically indicate this. Headings inform students of topics in advance if they will be reading the section; if they are doing research or choosing what to read, headings can help them decide.

28. A: Outcome. Story action can be analyzed in terms of rising action, story climax, falling action, and resolution. Rising action consists of those events that occur before and lead up to the story's most dramatic moment, or climax. The climax occurs toward the end of the book, but rarely, if ever, right at the end. Following the climax, the consequences of that dramatic moment are termed falling action. The story reaches the resolution with the outcome of the falling action.

29. D: Semantics refers to the meanings of words and language. The semantic system in the Three Cueing Systems model is the set of cues (including words, phrases, sentences, discourse, and complete text) that readers can use to recognize words based on meanings. Pragmatic cues (A) are based on reader purposes for reading and reader understanding of text structure. The phonological system (B) consists of cues related to the phonemic (or sound) structure of language. The syntactic system (C) consists of cues related to the sentence structure and word order of language.

30. A: It is important to evaluate specific reading skills, such as phonemic awareness, in a variety of contexts. Reading aloud with Abi allowed his teacher to notice that he consistently misread words beginning with digraphs. Digraphs are sounds in which two distinct letters, when combined, produce a single third sound (e.g. when "s" and "h" produce the "-sh" sound). Blends are words in which two letters produce a third sound which is a combination of both sounds put together (e.g. "b" and "l" combined to make "b"). The only set of words consisting only of digraphs is choice set "a."

31. D: Teachers should use a broad variety of instructional materials to support student vocabulary development, including not only literature and expository texts (A) but also newspapers, magazines (B), trade books, content-specific texts, technology (C), and other sources of vocabulary words to provide students with the richest and most authentic array of contexts possible for the greatest quantity and quality of exposure to and learning of vocabulary.

32. B: Revising. Revision (literally, re+vision) is the act of "seeing again." When revising, writers examine what they have written in order to improve the meaning of the work. Fine-tuning word choices, moving information to another location, and adding or deleting words are all acts of revision.

33. C: Thinking about thinking, or understanding our own cognitive processes, is known as metacognition. Explicitly teaching effective reading comprehension strategies does more than deepen student understanding of reading: it also promotes higher-order, abstract cognitive skill of metacognition. Schemata (A) (plural, singular *schema*) is Piaget's term for mental constructs we form to understand the world. Piaget said we either assimilate new information into an existing schema or alter an existing schema to accommodate the new knowledge. Reading instruction experts may refer to experience or background knowledge as schemata because students undergo this cognitive process when they fit what they read to their existing knowledge/experience. Scaffolding (B), a term coined by Jerome Bruner, means the temporary support given to students as needed while they learn and is gradually reduced as they become more independent. Reading instruction experts may also describe students' connections of text to prior experience as scaffolding. Metamorphosis (D) is a term meaning a transformation—literally in biology as with caterpillars into butterflies, or figuratively, as in Franz Kafka's *The Metamorphosis,* wherein protagonist Gregor Samsa becomes a cockroach.

34. B: Reading fluency combines accuracy, speed, and inflection while reading aloud. As children are learning to read, they work on all of these skills simultaneously with writing, thinking, viewing, listening, and comprehension. By using daily games or specific lessons, a teacher can directly affect students' ability to read the individual sounds in words (phonemes). As students identify more sounds correctly, they will read more accurately. Practicing reading aloud can increase fluency, but only if the child's reading partner is able to correct and encourage him or her to read more accurately. By reading aloud to the students, a teacher models correct speed and inflection, but this will affect the students' skills less directly than lessons and games in phonetics.

35. C: *Scribbling:* not printing, random; but significantly, representing ideas with written or drawn marks. *Letter-like symbols:* Forms resembling letters alternating with numbers, seldom with spacing. *Letter strings:* Some letters are legible, typically capitals, still not spaced; students mostly do not match letters to sounds yet but are developing phonological awareness. *Beginning sounds emerge:* Children still may not space between words, but begin distinguishing letters from words. Words match pictures, particularly with topics children choose. *Consonants represent words:* Children begin spacing between words, may mix upper-case and lower-case letters, start punctuating, and typically express ideas through written sentences. *Initial, middle, and final sounds:* Children may correctly spell familiar names, environmental print, and some sight words, but otherwise use spell phonetically; writing is much more readable. *Transitional phases:* Children's writing approximates conventional spelling. *Standard spelling:* Children spell most words correctly; they develop understanding of word roots, compound words, and contractions, increasing correct spelling of related words. (J. Richard Gentry, Ph.D., 1982, 2006, 2010)

36. D: A reader who identifies the emotions of characters in a story. Identifying the emotions of a character is not an element of metacognition. Metacognition means a reader's awareness of her own reading processes as she improves reading comprehension. Other elements of metacognition include awareness of areas in the text where the reader fails to comprehend and an understanding of how the text is structured.

37. C: Omitting articles (for example, *a/an, the, these*) and plural endings (*–s*), which is common among Chinese ESL students, is not because they have not yet learned the English forms (A) or words for these. Nor are these omissions a way to avoid having to choose the correct form among various English irregularities (C). These errors are also not due to the student's not understanding the relationship between the Chinese and English versions of the forms (D). Rather, Chinese does not include articles or plural endings the way English does, so the student has no frame of reference or comparison. Therefore, the student's ESL pattern of absent articles and plurals reflects the nature and rules of the L1, which have transferred to the L2 but are incompatible with it.

38. B: The intention of Round-robin reading is to provide practice reading aloud with appropriate fluency. This practice is also used to cover a large quantity of text with the entire class during the class period. By pairing the students, each child will get more practice reading aloud. He or she will also be more likely to stay engaged when working with only one partner, as there will be less time and fewer opportunities to become distracted. The teacher can then circulate amongst the groups to encourage focus and concentration, as well as provide guidance on fluency and comprehension of the text. As long as the students are paired carefully, this strategy is most likely preferable to the Round-robin method.

39. C: The best way for teachers to help students develop larger reading and writing vocabularies is simply to provide them with as many opportunities as possible for reading and writing. The more they read and write, the bigger their reading and writing vocabularies will grow, more effectively than from having to memorize vocabulary lists and being tested on them weekly (A). Having students search for new vocabulary words in texts (B) does not let them actually read, which is superior for learning new words within meaningful contexts as well as developing all other reading skills. Students learning new words in isolation will not learn their appropriate use. Rather than assigning minimum numbers of new words to include in their writing (D), teachers should give students actual opportunities to write, which both develops all writing skills and increases writing vocabulary. Also, choice B involves reading vocabulary but not writing vocabulary, and choice D involves writing vocabulary but not reading vocabulary, in addition to the fact that neither one involves actual reading and writing.

40. C: Persuasive. The author is hoping to persuade or convince readers to either request a pet and/or the primary care of their pet by providing them with facts as well as by using rhetorical devices such as dispelling opposing arguments.

41. B: In Old Italian, the word *disastro* meant unfavorable in one's stars. It was commonplace to attribute bad fortune to the influences of the stars in the Medieval and Renaissance eras. The Old Italian word came into English in the late 1500s as "disaster" and was used by Shakespeare (cf. *King Lear*). The word's Latin root is *astrum*, meaning "star," and the Latin prefix *dis-*, meaning "apart" and signifying negation. *Catastrophe* (A) and *misfortune* (C) are both Modern English meanings of the word "disaster," whereas the "ill-starred" meaning used in Elizabethan times has now become archaic or obsolete. The root means "star," not the aster flower (D).

42. B: Amelia exhibits some very specific symptoms in this vignette. She has trouble decoding sounds in words, cannot follow verbal directions or instructions, and displays both avoidance behaviors and oppositional behavior during difficult language tasks. All of these symptoms are characteristic of auditory processing problems in which a student cannot accurately and consistently understand written or verbally presented information. To a lesser extent, Amelia's symptoms may also suggest that she could have dyslexia, a reading disorder that affects the student's ability to read, write, do mathematics, or process information accurately. An educational specialist should be capable of pinpointing the causes of Amelia's difficulty.

43. A: News articles published on the worldwide web are more formal in their content and language than blogs on the web (B), which are written from a more personal, less journalistic perspective; or than email messages (C), which can be even more casual than blogs as they involve communications between individuals rather than writing intended for larger audiences like blogs and news articles. Hence, these are not all the same in formality level (D).

44. A: An Oral Reading Fluency assessment. ORF stands for oral reading fluency. This assessment measures the words correct per minute (WCPM) by subtracting the number of errors made from the total number of words orally read in a one-to-two-minute period of time. It is used to find a student's Instructional reading level, to identify readers who are having difficulties, and to track developing fluency and word recognition over time.

45. B: Typically, after students write something, their teachers may ask them to reflect upon what they wrote, which would mean that this is NOT a prewriting activity. In writing exercises, teachers will typically ask students to plan (A) what they will write in order to clearly define their main topic and organize their work. Many teachers find it helps students to visualize (C) what they are reading and/or want to write about and make drawings of what they visualize as preparation for writing. Brainstorming (D) is another common prewriting activity designed to generate multiple ideas from which students can then select to include in their writing.

46. B: Scaffolding refers to any kind of special instruction designed to help students learn a new or challenging concept. There are countless forms of scaffolding techniques. The three techniques mentioned in the question prompt are all used to facilitate student understanding of a given text or a concept taught within the text. Scaffolding should not be confused with modeling strategies, which refer to the process of demonstrating how something should be done before a student tries it on his or her own.

47. A: It is true that many students report grammar instruction as being "boring" or even irrelevant. However, knowledge of correct grammar can improve students' reading fluency, comprehension, writing, speaking, and other language skills. Therefore, it is important to help students understand the importance of learning grammatical rules and how they can be applied in various contexts. All language skills are interrelated and cannot be taught separately from one another since they evolve simultaneously. A skilled teacher will make grammar interesting by conveying its importance and finding innovative ways to incorporate fun activities into instruction.

48. C: Since the ratio of wages and benefits to other costs is 2:3, the amount of money spent on wages and benefits is $\frac{2}{5}$ of the business's total expenditure. $\frac{2}{5} \cdot \$130,000 = \$52,000$.

49. C: If x is a prime number and that the greatest common factor of x and y is greater than 1, the greatest common factor of x and y must be x. The least common multiple of two numbers is equal to the product of those numbers divided by their greatest common factor. So, the least common multiple of x and y is $\frac{xy}{x} = y$. Therefore, the values in the two columns are the same.

50. C: If 1" represents 60 feet, 10" represents 600 ft, which is the same as 200 yards.

51. D: Since all of the answer choices are parallelograms, determine whether the parallelogram is also a rhombus or a rectangle or both. One way to do this is by examining the parallelogram's diagonals. If the parallelogram's diagonals are perpendicular, then the parallelogram is a rhombus. If the parallelogram's diagonals are congruent, then the parallelogram is a rectangle. If a parallelogram is both a rhombus and a rectangle, then it is a square.

To determine whether the diagonals are perpendicular, find the slopes of the diagonals of the quadrilateral:

Diagonal 1: $\frac{6-2}{-5-3} = \frac{4}{-8} = -\frac{1}{2}$

Diagonal 2: $\frac{0-8}{-3-1} = -\frac{8}{-4} = 2$

The diagonals have opposite inverse slopes and are therefore perpendicular. Thus, the parallelogram is a rhombus.

To determine whether the diagonals are congruent, find the lengths of the diagonals of the quadrilateral:

Diagonal 1: $\sqrt{(6-2)^2 + (-5-3)^2} = \sqrt{(4)^2 + (-8)^2} = \sqrt{16 + 64} = \sqrt{80} = 4\sqrt{5}$

Diagonal 2: $\sqrt{(0-8)^2 + (-3-1)^{\wedge}2} = \sqrt{(-8)^2 + (-4)^{\wedge}2} = \sqrt{64 + 16} = \sqrt{80} = 4\sqrt{5}$

The diagonals are congruent, so the parallelogram is a rectangle.

Since the polygon is a rhombus and a rectangle, it is also a square.

52. A: Nominal data are data that are collected which have no intrinsic quantity or order. For instance, a survey might ask the respondent to identify his or her gender. While it is possible to compare the relative frequency of each response (for example, "most of the respondents are women"), it is not possible to calculate the mean, which requires data to be numeric, or median, which requires data to be ordered. Interval data are both numeric and ordered, so mean and median can be determined, as can the mode, the interval within which there are the most data. Ordinal data has an inherent order, but there is not a set interval between two points. For example, a survey might ask whether the respondent whether he or she was very dissatisfied, dissatisfied, neutral, satisfied, or very satisfied with the customer service received. Since the data are not numeric, the mean cannot be calculated, but since ordering the data is possible, the median has context.

53. A: The range is the spread of the data. It can be calculated for each class by subtracting the lowest test score from the highest, or it can be determined visually from the graph. The difference between the highest and lowest test scores in class A is 98-23=75 points. The range for each of the other classes is much smaller.

54. D: 75% of the data in a set is above the first quartile. Since the first quartile for this set is 73, there is a 75% chance that a student chosen at random from class 2 scored above a 73.

55. B: The number of students who like broccoli is equal to the number of students who like all three vegetables plus the number of students who like broccoli and carrots but not cauliflower plus the number of students who like broccoli and cauliflower but not carrots plus the number of students who like broccoli but no other vegetable: $3 + 15 + 4 + 10 = 32$. These students plus the numbers of students who like just cauliflower, just carrots, cauliflower and carrots, or none of the vegetables represents the entire set of students sampled: $32 + 2 + 27 + 6 + 23 = 90$. So, the probability that a randomly chosen student likes broccoli is $\frac{32}{90} \approx 0.356$.

The number of students who like carrots and at least one other vegetable is $15 + 6 + 3 = 24$. The number of students who like carrots is $24 + 27 = 51$. So, the probability that a student who likes carrots will also like at least one other vegetable is $\frac{24}{51} \approx 0.471$.

The number of students who like cauliflower and broccoli is $4 + 3 = 7$. The number of students who like all three vegetables is 3. So, the probability that a student who likes cauliflower and broccoli will also like carrots is $\frac{3}{7} \approx 0.429$.

The number of students who do not like carrots, broccoli, or cauliflower is 23. The total number of students surveyed is 90. So, the probability that a student does not like any of the three vegetables is 23/90 ≈ 0.256.

56. C: The original price may be represented by the equation $24{,}210 = x - 0.10x$ or $24{,}210 = 0.9x$. Dividing both sides of the equation by 0.9 gives $x = 26{,}900$.

57. A: The sum of 3 and the product of each term number and 5 equals the term value. For example, for term number 4, the value of 23 is equal to $5(4) + 3$, or 23.

58. C: The slope is equal to 4 since each ticket costs $4. The y-intercept is represented by the constant fee of $30. Substituting 4 for m and 30 for b into the equation $y = mx + b$ gives $y = 4x + 30$.

59. D: Since she spends at least $16, the relation of the number of packages of coffee to the minimum cost may be written as $4p \geq 16$. Alternatively, the inequality may be written as $16 \leq 4p$.

60. D: The cross-section of a cylinder will never be a triangle.

61. D: The number of outcomes in the event is 2 (rolling a 5 or 6), and the sample space is 6 (numbers 1 – 6). Thus, the probability may be written as $\frac{2}{6}$, which simplifies to $\frac{1}{3}$.

62. B: The students are more successful with physical objects. They can understand the concept of conservation. They can grasp subtraction in terms of concrete operations. Typically, 7-11 year olds are in the concrete operations stage. In this stage, the formal code is too abstract for their understanding. Therefore, the correct choice is B.

63. C: Since all of the teachers implementing a theme about the heart, this is a thematic unit. Collaborative learning typically involves students working in groups. Formative assessments are ways teachers assess learning while working on a unit. Differentiated instruction is the use of multiple methods when teaching a unit. Therefore, the correct choice is C.

64. A: In choice A, a comparison of the digits in the tenths place shows that 0.2 is greater than both 0.0499 and 0.007. Then, a comparison of the hundredths place shows that 0.0499 is greater than 0.007. Choice B should read $-2 < 0 < 7$. Choice C should read $\frac{1}{3} > \frac{1}{4} > \frac{1}{5}$. Choice D should read $-10 < -4 < -1$. Therefore, the correct choice is A.

65. D: The general form for this linear equation is $y = mx + b$ in which m is the jogger's rate and b is the jogger's distance from his front door at the beginning of his run. The rate can be found by $\frac{25.0-5.2}{3-0}$, which reduces to 6.6 meters per second. The starting distance from the door is 5.2 meters. The linear equation that represents this situation is $y = 6.6x + 5.2$.

Therefore, the correct choice is D.

66. C: A linear equation is an equation of the first degree. That means that the highest exponent of any term or variable is one, so it follows that an exponent cannot be variable. Choice C is a linear equation. Choices A and D are quadratic equations. Choice B is neither linear nor quadratic. Therefore, the correct choice is C.

67. D: A polygon may be decomposed into triangles by drawing all possible diagonals from one of the vertices. The sum of the degrees of a polygon is equal to the sum of the degrees of the triangles formed. Then the angle of the polygon is equal to that sum divided by the number of sides. For example, in a hexagon, four triangles are formed. The sum of the angles of a hexagon is equal to $4(180°)$ or $720°$. Each angle of a regular hexagon measures $\frac{720°}{6}$, or $120°$. Therefore, the correct choice is D.

68. C: This is a compound event. Since the marble is replaced after the first draw, the probability of each event is $\frac{1}{10}$. The probability of drawing two 5s in a row is $\frac{1}{10} \cdot \frac{1}{10}$ or $\frac{1}{100}$. Therefore, the correct choice is C.

69. B: If all primates are mammals, and all lemurs are primates, then all lemurs are mammals. All primates are not lemurs. Since neither whales nor monkeys are mentioned in the premises, they cannot be included in the conclusion. The conclusion can only be based on the information given in the premises. Therefore, the correct choice is B.

70. D: The set of integers is represented as $\{..., -3, -2, -1, 0, 1, 2, 3, ...\}$. The numbers 1, 2, 3, ..., are counting numbers, or natural numbers. Thus, the set contains the counting numbers, zero, and the negations of the counting numbers.

71. B: The situation may be modeled with the equation $\frac{1}{3} + \frac{1}{2} = \frac{1}{t}$, which simplifies to $\frac{5}{6} = \frac{1}{t}$. Thus, $t = \frac{6}{5}$. If working together, it will take them 1.2 hours to decorate the cake.

72. C: When two parallel lines are cut by a transversal, the consecutive angles formed inside the lines are supplementary.

73. D: The larger triangle has a base length of 3 units and a height of 3 units. The smaller triangle has a base length of 2 units and a height of 2 units. Thus, the dimensions of the larger triangle were multiplied by a scale factor of $\frac{2}{3}$. Note that $3 \cdot \left(\frac{2}{3}\right) = 2$.

74. A: The ends of Data Set A are farther apart, indicating a larger range. The horizontal line in the middle of a boxplot represents the median, so Data Set A also has a larger median.

75. C: If the rate of violent crimes per month is anything like it is the year before, it will be greatest in the summer months as there is a spike in the data on the 2005 graph during the summer months. While there is some fluctuation up and down throughout the entire year, these months are well beyond the numbers of the other months and represent the only upward trend in the graph.

76. B: The population is approximately 36,000, so one-quarter of the population consists of about 9,000 individuals under age 35. A third of 9,000 is 3,000, the approximate number of students in grades K-12. Since there are thirteen grades, there are about 230 students in each grade. So, the number of fourth graders is between 200 and 300.

77. A: The set of whole numbers, $\{0, 1, 2, 3, ...\}$, does not contain the number -4. Since -4 is an integer, it is also a rational number and a real number.

78. C:

$-4 \leq 2 + 3(x-1) \leq 2$	$-2x^2 + 2 \geq x^2 - 1$	$\dfrac{11 - \|3x\|}{7} \geq 2$	$3\|2x\| + 4 \leq 10$
$-6 \leq 3(x-1) \leq 0$	$-3x^2 \geq -3$	$11 - \|3x\| \geq 14$	$3\|2x\| \leq 6$
$-2 \leq x - 1 \leq 0$	$x^2 \leq 1$	$-\|3x\| \geq 3$	$\|2x\| \leq 2$
$-1 \leq x \leq 1$	$-1 \leq x \leq 1$	$\|3x\| \leq -1$	$-2 \leq 2x \leq 2$
		No solution	$-1 \leq x \leq 1$

79. C: When a figure is reflected twice over non-parallel lines, the resulting transformation is a rotation about the point of intersection of the two lines of reflection. The two lines of reflection $y = x + 2$ and $x = 0$ intersect at $(0,2)$. So, $\triangle A''B''C''$ represents a rotation of $\triangle ABC$ about the point

(0,2). The angle of rotation is equal to twice the angle between the two lines of reflection when measured in a clockwise direction from the first to the second line of reflection. Since the angle between the lines or reflection measures 135°, the angle of rotation which is the composition of the two reflections measures 270°. All of these properties can be visualized by drawing ΔABC, $\Delta A'B'C'$, and $\Delta A''B''C''$.

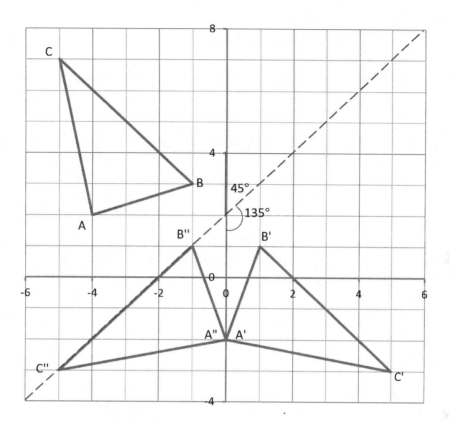

80. A: The average number of male students in the 11th and 12th grades is 125 $\left(\text{calculated as } \frac{131 + 119}{2}\right)$. The number of Hispanic students at the school is 10% of 1219, which is 122 students (rounded up from 121.9). The difference in the number of male and female students at the school is $630 - 589 = 41$, and the difference in the number of 9th and 12th grade students at the school is $354 - 255 = 99$.

81. C: 52% of the student population is white. There are 630 female students at the school out of 1219 students, so the percentage of female students is $\frac{630}{1219} \cdot 100\% \approx 52\%$. The percentages rounded to the nearest whole number are the same.

82. D: 131 of 283 eleventh graders are male. Given that an 11th grader is chosen to attend the conference, the probability that a male is chosen is $\frac{\text{number of males}}{\text{number of 11th graders}} = \frac{131}{283} \approx 0.46$. Note that this is **NOT** the same question as one which asks for the probability of selecting at random from the school a male student who is in eleventh grade, which has a probability of $\frac{131}{1219} \approx 0.11$.

83. C: The probability of an event is the number of possible occurrences of that event divided by the number of all possible outcomes. A camper who is at least eight years old can be eight, nine, or ten years old, so the probability of randomly selecting a camper at least eight years old

is $\frac{\text{number of eight-, nine-, and ten-year old campers}}{\text{total number of campers}} = \frac{14+12+10}{12+15+14+12+10} = \frac{36}{63} = \frac{4}{7}$.

84. C: His monthly salary may be modeled as $\frac{1}{8}x = 320$. Multiplying both sides of the equation by 8 gives $x = 2,560$.

85. D: All of these empires no longer existed following the armistice ending WWI. The Austro-Hungarian Empire (A), the Ottoman Empire (B), and the German Empire (C) were all among the Central powers that lost the war. As empires capitulated, armistices and peace treaties were signed and the map of Europe was redrawn as territories formerly occupied by Central powers were partitioned. For example, the former Austro-Hungarian Empire was partitioned into Austria, Hungary, Czechoslovakia, Yugoslavia, Transylvania, and Romania. The Treaty of Lausanne (1923) gave Turkey both independence and recognition as successor to the former Ottoman Empire after Turkey refused the earlier Treaty of Sèvres (1920), and Mustafa Kemal Ataturk led the Turkish Independence War. Greece, Bulgaria, and other former Ottoman possessions became independent. The Lausanne Treaty defined the boundaries of these countries as well as the boundaries of Iraq, Syria, Cyprus, Sudan, and Egypt.

86. C: A caucus is a private event run by political parties, and a primary is an indirect election run by state and local governments. Voters may award delegates to candidates for the national conventions, depending on state laws.

87. D: According to Article III of the Constitution, Justices of the Supreme Court, judges of the courts of appeals and district courts, and judges of the Court of International Trade are appointed by the President with the confirmation of the Senate. The judicial branch of the government is the only one not elected by the people.

88. C: Hernando Cortes conquered the Mexican Aztecs in 1519. He had several advantages over the Indians, including horses, armor for his soldiers, and guns. In addition, Cortes' troops unknowingly transmitted smallpox to the Aztecs, which devastated their population as they had no immunity to this foreign illness. Vasco Nunez de Balboa (A) was the first European explorer to view the Pacific Ocean when he crossed the Isthmus of Panama in 1513. Juan Ponce de Leon (B) also visited and claimed Florida in Spain's name in 1513. Cabeza de Vaca (D) was one of only four men out of 400 to return from an expedition led by Panfilio de Narvaez in 1528 and was responsible for spreading the story of the Seven Cities of Cibola (the "cities of gold"). Hernando de Soto led an expedition from 1539-1541 to the southeastern part of America.

89. D: These are all true. Because the Puritans took on a Reformed theology, they were in this sense Calvinists (A). However, many Puritans endorsed radical views that criticized such Calvinists as founder John (Jean) Calvin and Huldrych (Ulrich) Zwingli in Switzerland. Not only were Puritans critical of Calvinists despite their mutual Reformed approaches, reciprocally many Calvinists were opposed to the Puritans as well (C). The Puritan movement changed less in American colonies than in England during the 1660s. Following the Restoration (1660) and the Uniformity Act (1662) in England, nearly all of the Puritan clergy objected and left the Church of England, thereby creating a dramatic change in the movement in that country. Nevertheless, in America, the Puritans who had emigrated from England continued their original Puritan traditions for a longer time, as they had neither the same Anglican Church as in England nor the legislation restoring earlier church status against which the English Puritans had reacted.

90. B: Keynesian economics is based on the notion that governments can effectively stimulate economic growth through taxation, adjustment of interest rates, and the funding of public projects. His economic philosophy contrasts sharply with the free-market philosophies of Smith, Hayek, and Friedman.

91. B: Congress has the authority to shape the judicial branch. The Supreme Court once operated with only six members. Nine has been the standard number since 1869.

92. B: The first amendment to the Constitution states, "Congress shall make no law respecting an establishment of religion, or prohibiting the free exercise thereof; or abridging the freedom of speech or of the press; or the right of the people peaceably to assemble, and to petition the Government for a redress of grievances." The right to bear arms is guaranteed by the second amendment: "A well-regulated Militia, being necessary to the security of a free State, the right of the people to keep and bear Arms, shall not be infringed."

93. B: Diversity is not one of the demographic variables. Demographers, or those who study population, rely on fertility, mortality, and migration to determine the number of people in a region. The general equation is *Total Population = Original Population + Births – Deaths + Immigration – Emigration*. The natural increase, on the other hand, is calculated only with the number of births and deaths. The diversity of a population may be relevant to subsequent research performed by the demographer, but it is not considered one of the essential three demographic variables.

94. B: John Maynard Keynes argued that government could help revitalize a recessionary economy by increasing government spending and therefore increasing aggregate demand. This is known as demand-side economics.

95. C: The bubonic plague spread along trade routes, carried by infected animals and people on ships. After reaching Cyprus in 1347, the epidemic followed trade routes to infect the populations of Italy and France. Then, also through trade routes, it traveled north to Germany, England, and eventually Scandinavia and Russia in 1351.

96. D: Political corruption was not an immediate effect of the rapid urban growth during this time. The accelerated growth of cities in America did soon result in services being unable to keep up with that growth. The results of this included deficiencies in clean water delivery and garbage collection, causing poor sanitation (A). That poor sanitation led to outbreaks of cholera and typhus, as well as typhoid fever epidemics (B). Police and firefighting services could not keep up with the population increases, and were often inadequate (C). With people moving to the cities at such a fast rate, there were also deficits in housing and public transportation.

97. D: Increases in population growth supplied additional labor forces, helping to enable the Industrial Revolution. These increases were due to the prosperity brought through Europe's Commercial Revolution, which preceded the Industrial Revolution. The rediscovery of concrete, new advances in iron making, and the invention of the steam engine are all examples of developments that occurred during the Industrial Revolution.

98. B: As production shifted to factories, a large number of unskilled workers were needed to operate the machinery that was beginning to put many skilled craftsmen out of work. As farms grew larger and increasingly mechanized, the number of people who owned their own farm began to decrease. The rural population declined as people flocked to the cities in search of employment.

99. D: Free public education has been a U.S. tradition since the 18th century. State constitutions govern the education issues of each state, although federal, state, and local governments all work together on educational issues.

100. C: The person or group *not* instrumental in advancing civil rights and desegregation immediately after WWII was (C), Congress. As African American soldiers came home from the war, racial discord increased. President Harry Truman (A) appointed a Presidential Committee on Civil Rights in 1946. This committee published a report recommending that segregation and lynching be outlawed by the federal government. However, Congress ignored this report and took no action. Truman then used his presidential powers to enforce desegregation of the military and policies of "fair employment" in federal civil service jobs. The National Association for the Advancement of Colored People (NAACP) (D) brought lawsuits against racist and discriminatory practices, and in resolving these suits, the Supreme Court (B) further eroded segregation. For example, the Supreme Court ruled that primaries allowing only whites would be illegal, and it ended the segregation of interstate bus lines. The landmark civil rights laws were not passed by Congress until the 1960s

101. A: The Industrial Revolution did create a new working class composed of professionals like doctors and lawyers, industrialists, and businessmen. Formerly, Europe was dominated by royalty and landed gentry over the poor working class. Industrialization allowed many ordinary people to start and run businesses. It did NOT, however, improve working conditions in the 18th and early 19th centuries, but the opposite occurred: Big factories with machines made conditions more dangerous, and child labor caused many deaths, injuries, illnesses, and so on. Women and children were only banned from working in mines in the mid-19th century; housing and work conditions only improved in the late 19th century. Urbanization was the result of industrialization and not vice versa: Mechanization allowed factory construction, and people moved to cities for jobs. Labor unions developed out of the Industrial Revolution, not vice versa, to establish and defend factory workers' rights.

102. B: The Supreme Court ruled that statements made in interrogation are not admissible unless the defendant is informed of the right to an attorney and waives that right. The case of Miranda v. Arizona was consolidated with Westover v. United States, Vignera v. New York, and California v. Stewart.

103. A: As people have more and more of something, they value it less and less. This is the law of diminishing marginal utility, and it is what causes the downward slope of the demand curve.

104. A: Agriculture was not a viable economic model for New Englanders. Although the colonists were mainly from England and Scotland, few were merchants before arriving in the colonies. Slavery existed in the north, although it was less important to the economy than it was in the agricultural south. New England colonists were not actively competing with their neighbors to the immediate south.

105. B: Followers of Hinduism, an indigenous religion of India, believes in one Supreme Reality (Brahman), manifested in many different gods and goddesses that oversee different aspects of life. Confucianism, a Chinese religion, does not address whether there are many gods or one. Followers of Sikhism, an Indian religion originating in Punjab, believe in a single god, Om or Ik Om Kar. Islam, founded by Muhammad in Saudi Arabia, purports a single god, Allah.

106. A: The President of the United States serves as Commander-in-Chief, but the writers of the Constitution, who feared how authority was used by monarchs, limited the President's power in this role. The President cannot declare war or oversee military regulations, although Presidents have traditionally authorized the use of force without war being declared.

107. A: When the prices farmers receive for their crops decline in a developing country, this typically results in increased urbanization. When crop prices decline, farmers can no longer make a living from their land. As a result, they often choose to migrate to cities in search of low-wage employment in the manufacturing or service sectors.

108. B: It is not true that the Crusades succeeded at Christians' reclaiming the "holy land" (the Middle East) from Muslims. Despite their number (nine not counting the Northern Crusades) and longevity (1095-1291 not counting later similar campaigns), the Crusades never accomplished this purpose (A). While they did not take back the Middle East, the Crusades did succeed in exacerbating the decline of the Byzantine Empire (C), which lost more and more territory to the Ottoman Turks during this period. In addition, the Crusades resulted in Egypt's rise once again to become a major power (D) of the Middle East as it had been in the past. It is also true that during the Crusades, some Christians and Muslims became allies against common enemies. For example, during the Fifth Crusade, in Anatolia, Christian Crusaders with German, Dutch, Flemish, and Frisian soldiers allied themselves with the Sultanate of Rûm, a Seljuk Turk Sultanate that attacked the Ayyubids in Syria, in order to further their aim of attacking and capturing the port of Damietta in Egypt.

109. C: Nebraska does not require voter registration, but all other states do and have their own process. State and local officials administer federal elections, and though each state has its own method for holding elections, federal elections are always held at the same time.

110. A: Anyone may write a bill, but only a member of Congress can introduce a bill. The President often suggests bills. Bills can change drastically throughout the review process.

111. C: The chaparral biome features scrubby plants and small evergreen trees and also has a hot, dry summer followed by a wetter winter. This biome is mainly found around the Mediterranean Sea, though there are also chaparrals in Australia, South Africa, and the American Southwest. The taiga is a colder biome found primarily in northern Europe and Asia. The vegetation of the taiga is mainly scattered stands of coniferous trees. A coniferous forest, meanwhile, is a warmer forest composed of trees that have needles and cones rather than leaves. These trees are better suited for a cold climate than are deciduous trees. A savanna is a tropical grassland with only a few trees. Savannas are clustered around the equator.

112. C: Exploration between the 15th and 17th centuries resulted in contact between European cultures and many previously unknown or little-known cultures. Navigation techniques improved, food and other goods were imported, and the New World began to be settled. Rather than declining in influence, England became a more prominent imperial power during this era.

113. A: Glaciers move because they are incredibly heavy, and the force of gravity slowly pulls them lower. Erosion is a result rather than a cause of glacier movement. Although large glaciers may only move a few inches a year or may not move at all, some valley glaciers in Europe move as much as 600 feet annually. The result is a rounded valley and a trail of rock and soil debris known as a moraine. The Great Lakes in the United States were formed by the passage of glaciers long ago.

114. D: Destructive interference. Destructive interference describes two waves that are out of phase as they come together to produce a new wave. Out of phase refers to the crest of one and the trough of another arriving together. Interference, when used to discuss wave phenomenon, is the interaction of two or more waves passing the same point, which could be either destructive or constructive. Incomplete interference and distorted interference are not real terms. Constructive interference refers to wave interference that results in higher peaks than the waves singularly because the waves arrive in phase with one another (the crests arrive together).

115. B: Stomata. A stoma is the part of a plant system that responds to stimuli by releasing water via transpiration. It can also close during adverse conditions like a drought to prevent the plant from dehydration. Stomata closure can also be triggered by the presence of bacteria. Pith refers to the central, spongy part of the stem in vascular plants. Guard cells flank stomata and regulate the opening. Sepals are modified leaves that protect the flower bud before it opens.

116. A: Phase changes are physical changes, not chemical changes (B). Sublimation (C) occurs when a solid turns directly into a gas without passing through the liquid state. Condensation (D) occurs when a gas turns to liquid.

117. A: By multiplying the ocular lens power times the objective being used. When using a light microscope, total magnification is determined by multiplying the ocular lens power times the objective being used. The ocular lens refers to the eyepiece, which has one magnification strength, typically 10x. The objective lens also has a magnification strength, often 4x, 10x, 40x or 100x. Using a 10x eyepiece with the 4x objective lens will give a magnification strength of 40x. Using a 10x eyepiece with the 100x objective lens will give a magnification strength of 1,000x. The shorter lens is the lesser magnification; the longer lens is the greater magnification.

118. B: The air we breathe is composed of many types of molecules, and is quite heavy compared to helium. The reason helium balloons float is because helium is less dense than the surrounding air. Objects that are less dense will float in objects that are more dense, as a helium balloon does when surrounded by air.

119. D: Glaciers. Glaciers and ice caps are fresh water unavailable for human use as they are frozen. The hydrologic cycle refers to all the water on planet Earth. Some water is in forms that humans do not tend to use, such as oceans (too salty and expensive to desalinate) and glaciers. Water suitable for drinking can be found as surface water and in ground water, which is obtained through wells. Rivers, Estuaries, and Aquifers are all examples of surface water that are available to humans.

120. C: A physical change occurs when water condenses. The only thing formed during condensation is new intermolecular bonds. Therefore, no new covalent bonds form (B). The only time new atoms form is during a nuclear reaction (A). The water molecule is not ionizing, so no new ionic bonds form (D).

121. D: Temperature. The amount of potential energy an object has depends on mass, height above ground and gravitational attraction, but not temperature. The formula for potential energy is PE = mgh, or potential energy equals mass times gravity times height. Answers A, B, and C are all valid answers as they are all contained in the formula for potential energy. Potential energy is the amount of energy stored in a system particularly because of its position.

122. D: The molecules that make up gases are far apart and move about very quickly. Because they have a weak attraction to each other, they expand to take up as much space as possible.

123. B: Two crustal plates move apart. When two crustal plates move apart, magma welling up could result in the formation of new crust. This has been shown to be occurring on the ocean floor where places of the crust are weaker. The crust spreads apart at these trenches, pushing outward and erupting at the ridges. When two crustal plates converge, sublimation occurs as one plate runs under another pushing it up. Two crustal plates sliding past one another is an example of a transform fault, which does not create new crust. A crustal plate being pushed down into the mantle does not form new crust but perhaps recycles the old one.

124. A: The purpose of conducting an experiment is to test a hypothesis. Choices B, C, and D are steps in conducting an experiment designed to test a hypothesis.

125. B: Conduction. A long nail or other type of metal, substance or matter that is heated at one end and then the other end becomes equally hot is an example of conduction. Conduction is energy transfer by neighboring molecules from an area of hotter temperature to cooler temperature. Radiation, or thermal radiation, refers to heat being transferred without the need for a medium by electromagnetic radiation. An example is sunlight heating the earth. Convection refers to heat being transferred by molecules moving from one location in the substance to another creating a heat current, usually in a gas or a liquid. Entropy relates to the second law of thermodynamics and refers to how much heat or energy is no longer available to do work in a system. It can also be stated as the amount of disorder in a system.

126. C: High concentration. A higher concentration could increase the reaction rate of a chemical reaction. The rate of reaction is affected by concentration, pressure and temperature. A higher concentration would allow for more potential collisions that set off the reaction. Low kinetic energy would lead to a lower rate of reaction, as does a lower temperature (usually). The term activation energy refers to the specific threshold that must be overcome for a reaction to occur. If the activation energy is lowered, for example, by a catalyst or enzyme, then the reaction can occur quicker. This rules out high activation energy.

127. B: A footprint. A trace fossil is that which shows evidence of existence but is not an organism itself. A trace fossil can be contrasted with a body fossil, which has been formed from an organism. Other examples of trace fossils include eggs, nests, burrows, borings and coprolites (fossilized feces). A mouse jaw and a shark tooth are examples of body fossils. A cast of a skull is a replica and neither a body nor a trace fossil.

128. A: When two tectonic plates are moving laterally in opposing directions, this is called a transform boundary. When there is friction at transform boundaries and pressure builds up, it can result in shallow earthquakes (usually at a depth of less than 25 meters). California's San Andreas Fault is an example of a transform boundary.

129. D: It is a stable atom. If an atom's outer shell is filled, it is a stable atom. The outer shell refers to one of many energy levels, or shells, that electrons occupy around a nucleus. An atom whose outer shell is not filled wants to become stable by filling the outer shell. It fills its outer shell by forming bonds. The atom can do this by gaining electrons or losing electrons in ionic compounds, or if the atom is a part of a molecule, by sharing electrons. If an atom has a full outer shell, such as the noble gases, it does not readily react with other atoms and does not exchange electrons to form bonds. These atoms are known as inert. Therefore, Answers A and B cannot be true. Answer C, It has 32 electrons in its outer shell, is not necessarily true because not all elements have the fourth shell that can hold 32 electrons. Some have fewer shells that hold fewer electrons.

130. D: Non-polar. A non-polar substance is least likely to be soluble in water. A rule of thumb for a substance's solubility is that like dissolves like. Polarity is affected by the types of bonds between atoms and the bonds are affected by the types of atoms. An unequal sharing of electrons leads to polar bonding and polar substances. Water is polar and can dissolve many other polar substances. Hydrophilic molecules are polar and this word means "water-loving". Water also dissolves many ionic substances since they are composed of charged ions and can interact with the polar water molecules. Many organic compounds are non-polar and do not dissolve well in water.

131. B: Cold water dissolves atmospheric carbon dioxide, stores it, and releases it back out to the atmosphere as needed. This describes the physical or non-biological part of the carbon cycle. The carbon and nutrient cycles of the ocean are processed in part by the deep currents, mixing, and upwelling that occurs. Carbon dioxide (CO_2) from the atmosphere is dissolved into the ocean at the higher latitudes and distributed to the denser deep water. When upwelling occurs, CO_2 is brought back to the surface and emitted into the tropical air.

132. D: After a secondary consumer dies, such as a wolf, its body is partially consumed by decomposers, such as bacteria and fungi. Bacteria and fungi live in soil and digest body tissues of dead organisms converting them into basic nutrients that plants need to grow. Therefore, after secondary consumers die, their energy is consumed by decomposers, who make nutrients available in the soil for producers to use. *Do not confuse nutrients in the soil with energy that producers get from the Sun to make their own food.*

133. A: Heat between objects in contact with each other is transferred by conduction, choice A: Convection is transfer by currents within a body of fluid, and radiation is the transfer of heat between objects *not* in contact, through light rays emitted by the hotter object and absorbed by the cooler one.

134. A: Cytoplasm. The type of RNA described by the question is transfer RNA (tRNA). The tRNA is found in the cytoplasm and carries and positions amino acids at the ribosome for protein synthesis. There are two other types of RNA. Messenger RNA (mRNA) contains the coding for the amino acid sequence in the protein. The mRNA is first made in the nucleus before traveling through the cytoplasm to a ribosome. Ribosomal RNA (rRNA) is the RNA that is found in the ribosome along with proteins, which allows the mRNA and tRNA to bind for protein synthesis. All three types of RNA originate in the nucleus where they are transcribed from DNA. Mitochondria are organelles that harbor mitochondrial DNA (mtDNA).

135. B: Venus. Venus experiences a greenhouse effect similar to that observed on Earth as its dense atmosphere traps the solar radiation and creates a greenhouse effect. The greenhouse gasses, including ozone, carbon dioxide, water vapor and methane, trap infrared radiation that is reflected back toward the atmosphere. Human activity generates more of the greenhouse gasses than necessary. Some practices that increase the amount of greenhouse gasses are burning natural gas and oil, farming, which leads to more methane and nitrous oxide, deforestation, which decreases the amount of offset oxygen, and population growth in general, which increases the volume of greenhouse gasses. Increased gasses mean more infrared radiation is trapped and the overall temperature at the Earth's surface rises.

136. B: The energy radiated by stars is produced by nuclear fusion. This is the process whereby the nuclei of individual atoms bind together to form heavier elements and release energy outward. By the time this energy, which is created in the star's core, reaches the outer walls of the star, it exists in the form of light.

137. A: The charge on the glass rod is positive and the charge on the cloth is negative when the glass rod is rubbed with a cloth made of polyester. This is an example of static electricity — the collection of electrically charged particles on the surface of a material. A static charge can be quickly discharged, commonly called a "spark", or discharged more slowly by dissipating to the ground. A static charge occurs because different materials have a capacity for giving up electrons and becoming positive (+), or for attracting electrons and becoming negative (-). The triboelectric series is a list of materials and their propensities for either giving up electrons to become positive or to gain the electrons to become negative. Polyester has a tendency to gain electrons to become negative and glass has a tendency to lose electrons to become positive.

138. B: They use tube feet for locomotion and feeding. Animals belonging to the phylum Echinodermata have tube feet for locomotion and feeding. About 7,000 species are extant in this phylum, including starfish and sand dollars. Tube feet are an organ system that provides locomotion, respiration, feeding and sensory functions. Not all echinoderms have appendages. Having an exoskeleton made of chitin is characteristic of arthropods. Not all echinoderms must shed their outer layer of skin to grow.

139. B: An iron bar moving inside a coil of wire that contains a current would create an electromagnet. Choice C creates an electric current. Choice D creates the Earth's magnetic field.

140. D: Gravitational collapse and high-energy collisions are both proposed explanations for the formation of black holes. Gravitational collapse occurs when the outward pressure exerted by an object is too weak to resist that object's own gravity. Collisions that produce conditions of sufficient density could also, in theory, create black holes. The accretion of matter is considered observational evidence for the existence of black holes.

Practice Test #2

1. Research has found which of the following outcomes occur for students via revision and rewriting?

    a. Students only correct their mechanical errors in revisions.
    b. Students often incorporate new ideas when they rewrite.
    c. Students retain their original writing goals during revision.
    d. Students' planning in prewriting is unaffected in rewriting.

2. With a teacher's guidance, a class brainstorms main ideas, topics, or concepts from a text. Students choose a select number of these ideas and copy them onto separate index cards. The students then individually review the text, recording any supporting evidence on the notecard with the applicable main idea. This activity would be an excellent pre-lesson for teaching which skill set?

    a. Working as a group to interpret a text and write an appropriate and realistic sequel, focusing on interpretive comprehension and creative writing.
    b. Silent reading as a form of comprehension practice.
    c. Organizing ideas for writing a cohesive and persuasive essay or research paper that asserts supported arguments with valid supporting evidence.
    d. Literal and figurative comprehension, as well as contributing to group discussions via oral communication skills.

3. A teacher is working with a group of third graders at the same reading level. Her goal is to improve reading fluency. She asks each child in turn to read a page from a book about mammal young. She asks the children to read with expression. She also reminds them they don't need to stop between each word; they should read as quickly as they comfortably can. She cautions them, however, not to read so quickly that they leave out or misread a word. The teacher knows the components of reading fluency are:

    a. Speed, drama, and comprehension
    b. Cohesion, rate, and prosody
    c. Understanding, rate, and prosody
    d. Rate, accuracy, and prosody

4. *Caret, carrot, to, two and too* share something in common. They:

    a. Are nouns
    b. Are monosyllabic
    c. Are homophones
    d. Represent things in nature

5. Of the following statements, which adheres to Information Literacy standards?

    a. Students accessing information must critically evaluate it and its sources before using it.
    b. Students accessing information can ascertain how much of it they need after they find it.
    c. Students accessing information efficiently sacrifice broader scope and incidental learning.
    d. Students accessing information ethically must eschew using it to attain specific purposes.

6. Third-grade students typically receive their spelling word lists each Monday so that they can practice them at home before the test on Friday. While their teacher is pleased that the students usually receive high grades on spelling tests she observes that they misspell those same words when writing in journals or doing classwork. How should this teacher modify her instruction?

    a. Post a list of vocabulary words when the students are writing to help them recall correct spellings.

    b. Integrate spelling words into writing, reading, grammar, phonics, and other activities to help students learn the words in a variety of contexts.

    c. Provide more time, such as a two-week period, between tests so that students have more time to study.

    d. Review the words before certain activities to increase immediate recall of correct spellings.

7. Of the three tiers of words, the most important words for direct instruction are:

    a. Tier-one words

    b. Common words

    c. Tier-two words

    d. Words with Latin roots

8. Which student is most likely to need referral to a reading specialist for assessment, special instruction, or intervention?

    a. Annabel: a 2nd-grade student who tends to skip over words or phrases when she reads, affecting her comprehension of the text

    b. Cliff: a kindergarten student who is already reading simple chapter books with his parents at home or in class

    c. Noelle: a 1st-grader who avoids any activity in which she must read, both aloud and silently, preferring to ask an adult to read the text for her first

    d. Barrett: a 3rd-grader who often confuses the sounds of certain letters, such as /b/ and /d/ or /v/ and /u

9. The MLA guidelines for citing multiple authors of the same source in the in-text citations of a research paper are to use the first author's name and "et al" for the other(s) in the case of…

    a. More than one author.

    b. Two or three authors.

    c. Three or more authors.

    d. Four or more authors.

10. A child in kindergarten is *most* likely to be referred to a speech-language pathologist if s/he does not correctly produce which of the following phonemes?

    a. /p/ as in pepper or poppies

    b. /ʒ/ as in mirage or measure

    c. /v/ as in velvet, valve, value

    d. /s/ as in see, yes, or asking

11. Which of the following best explains the importance prior knowledge brings to the act of reading?

a. Prior knowledge is information the student gets through researching a topic prior to reading the text. A student who is well-prepared through such research is better able to decode a text and retain its meaning.

b. Prior knowledge is knowledge the student brings from previous life or learning experiences to the act of reading. It is not possible for a student to fully comprehend new knowledge without first integrating it with prior knowledge.

c. Prior knowledge is predictive. It motivates the student to look for contextual clues in the reading and predict what is likely to happen next.

d. Prior knowledge is not important to any degree to the act of reading because every text is self-contained and therefore seamless. Prior knowledge is irrelevant in this application.

12. A fourth-grade teacher had her students write haiku in order to promote the students' _____.

a. Reading comprehension
b. Vocabulary
c. Word identification skills
d. Confidence

13. What is a mnemonic device?

a. A saying or image used to help remember a complex concept
b. A tool that increases physical relaxation during a test
c. An old-fashioned torture device involving repeated testing
d. A tool for selecting answers on tests

14. Of the following, which statement is true about instruction in the alphabetic principle?

a. Letter-sound relationships with the highest utility should be the earliest ones introduced.
b. The instruction of letter-sound correspondences should always be done in word context.
c. Letter-sound relationship practice times should only be assigned apart from other lessons.
d. Letter-sound relationship practice should focus on new relationships, not go over old ones.

15. All members of a group of kindergarten students early in the year are able to chant the alphabet. The teacher is now teaching the students what the alphabet looks like in written form. The teacher points to a letter and the students vocalize the correspondent sound. Alternatively, the teacher vocalizes a phoneme and a student points to it on the alphabet chart. The teacher is using _____ in her instruction.

a. Letter–sound correspondence
b. Rote memorization
c. Predictive analysis
d. Segmentation

16. Components of "explicit instruction" include:

a. Clarifying the goal, modeling strategies, and offering explanations geared to a student's level of understanding

b. Determining the goal, offering strategies, and asking questions designed to ascertain whether understanding has been reached

c. Reassessing the goal, developing strategies, and determining whether further reassessing of the goal is required

d. Objectifying the goal, assessing strategies, and offering explanations geared toward a student's level of understanding.

17. _____ is the overall choice of language you make for your writing; _____ are the specific words from a given discipline that you use when writing within or about that discipline.

a. Vocabulary; diction

b. Vocabulary; jargon

c. Diction; vocabulary

d. Style; vocabulary

18. Regarding these elements of print awareness in literacy development, which is true?

a. All students with normal development can differentiate printed words from spaces.

b. To identify initial and final letters in words, students must identify words vs. spaces.

c. The only students not automatically knowing left-right directionality are certain ELLs.

d. Being able to identify basic punctuation is not important to reading comprehension.

19. It is the beginning of the school year. To determine which second-grade students might need support, the reading teacher wants to identify those who are reading below grade level. She works with students one at a time. She gives each child a book at a second-grade reading level and asks the child to read out loud for two minutes. Children who will need reading support are those who read:

a. Fewer than 50 words in the time given

b. Fewer than 150 words in the time given

c. More than 75 words in the time given

d. The entire book in the time given

20. When working with English Language Learners, the teacher should:

a. Avoid idioms and slang, involve students in hands-on activities, reference students' prior knowledge, and speak slowly

b. Speak slowly, use monosyllabic words whenever possible, repeat each sentence three times before moving to the next sentence, and employ idioms but not slang

c. Use monosyllabic words whenever possible, repeat key instructions three times but not in a row, reference students' prior knowledge, and have students keep a journal of new vocabulary

d. Have students keep a journal of new vocabulary, speak normally, and try not to treat the students differently because of their previous experiences

21. Which of the following processes used in writing is the most complex?

a. Evaluation

b. Application

c. Comprehension

d. Knowledge recall

22. When a teacher instructs elementary school students in analyzing phonetically regular words, which of the following would most represent a sequence from simpler to progressively more complex?

    a. Long vowels, short vowels, consonant blends, CVC (consonant-vowel-consonant) and other common patterns, individual phonemes, blending phonemes, types of syllables, onsets and rimes

    b. Onsets and rimes, short vowels, consonant blends, long vowels, blending phonemes, CVC and other common patterns, types of syllables, individual phonemes

    c. Types of syllables, onsets and rimes, CVC and other common patterns, consonant blends, blending phonemes, individual phonemes, long vowels, short vowels

    d. Individual phonemes, blending phonemes, onsets and rimes, short vowels, long vowels, consonant blends, CVC and other common patterns, types of syllables

23. Which text(s) are likely to foster the greatest enthusiasm for and increase comprehension in reading and literature among students?

    a. An all-in-one textbook that includes all reading material for the year, study guides, and sample test questions

    b. A small range of texts with common content, format, and difficulty

    c. A variety of texts, including books, magazines, newspapers, stories from oral traditions, poetry, music, and films

    d. A small selection of current best-selling books for children, some of which the children may already have read and liked

24. "Coarticulation" affects:

    a. Blending awareness
    b. Phonemic awareness
    c. Sequencing
    d. Aural awareness

25. Some of the students in Mr. Smith's fourth-grade class cannot decode words well enough to read fluently in class. He knows they are well behind grade level and that he needs to provide them with activities that will allow them to be successful, building skills and confidence at the same time. Which activity would be best for this purpose?

    a. Enlist the parents' help by sending home a weekly list of sight words that the students can practice and memorize, decreasing the need to decode when they read.

    b. Show the students how to create words out of movable alphabet tiles or magnetic letters, building (encoding) words as they sound them out.

    c. Provide the children with early childhood readers that contain only very simple words so that the children will not feel bad as they read.

    d. Allow those children having trouble to stop each time they reach a challenging word and sound it out carefully, recording it to a list that will be studied for homework.

26. Which of the following involves evaluative reading comprehension?

    a. Identifying an author's point of view
    b. Explaining the author's point of view
    c. Identifying the main idea of the text
    d. Predicting what will happen in a text

27. *Since, whether,* and *accordingly* are examples of which type of signal words?
    a. Common, or basic, signal words
    b. Compare/contrast words
    c. Cause–effect words
    d. Temporal sequencing words

28. In the Three Cueing Systems model of word recognition in reading instruction, which system most relates to how words are assembled into meaningful language?
    a. Phonological
    b. Semantic
    c. Syntactic
    d. Pragmatic

29. Which adult would be most effective in helping a student who frequently mispronounces sounds both in reading and in conversation?
    a. A whole language specialist
    b. A speech pathologist
    c. A paraprofessional
    d. A psychologist

30. Of the following, which represents an indirect way in which students receive instruction in and learn vocabulary?
    a. Being exposed repeatedly to vocabulary in multiple teaching contexts
    b. Being exposed to vocabulary when adults read aloud to them
    c. Being pre-taught specific words found in text prior to reading
    d. Being taught vocabulary words over extended periods of time

31. A teacher is teaching students analogizing. She is teaching them to:
    a. Identify and use metaphors
    b. Identify and use similes
    c. Identify and use groups of letters that occur in a word family
    d. Identify and use figures of speech

32. Scholars have identified three kinds of major connections that students make when reading: connecting text to self, text to the world, and text to text. Which of the following student statements best reflect(s) the connection of text to the world?
    a. "These mythic gods have more power, but feel and act like humans."
    b. "This novel is set during a period I learned about in my history class."
    c. "I can relate to how the main character felt about being controlled."
    d. All three statements equally reflect connection of text to the world.

33. Learning to construct a reading response would be most beneficial in enhancing which language skill?
    a. Oral presentation
    b. Comprehension
    c. Fluency
    d. Learning a second language

34. Which of the following ways of presenting information is best for showing change over time?

    a. Tables
    b. Maps
    c. Graphs
    d. Charts

35. A teacher is working with a student who is struggling with reading. The teacher gives him a story with key words missing:

    > The boy wanted to take the dog for a walk. The boy opened the door. The ____ ran out. The ___ looked for the dog. When he found the dog, he was very _____.

The student is able to fill in the blanks by considering:

    a. Syntax. Often, word order gives enough clues that a reader can predict what happens next.
    b. Pretext. By previewing the story, the student can deduce the missing words.
    c. Context. By considering the other words in the story, the student can determine the missing words.
    d. Fallacies. By checking for common errors of thought, the student can determine the missing words.

36. Which statement is most accurate about social contexts of L1 and L2 acquisition?

    a. Both L1 and L2 learning can occur in equally varied natural and educational contexts.
    b. L1s are only learned in natural contexts, while L2s are learned in educational contexts.
    c. Variations in L2 proficiency can result from the different contexts of learning the L2s.
    d. L2s are not a speaker's natural language and so are never learned in natural contexts.

37. Which of the following choices would be the best comprehensive project for a 4th-grade class at the end of the school year?

    a. An open-book, cumulative test that measures the students' understanding of various concepts and genres through multiple choice, short-answer, and short-essay questions.
    b. Assign children to a group in which they will read and adapt a short play. Each group will perform its play with costumes and staging while the rest of the class will serve as audience members. Audience members will write short responses to what they have seen, which will be shared with the performers.
    c. Each student picks a topic about which they would like to conduct independent research. The students will read a variety of texts from different sources to learn more about the topic and then use that information to create a presentation for the class. The use of technology and media is encouraged in presentations.
    d. The students take a field trip to the local university to visit the English Department. The students are permitted to sit in on a class lecture and speak to professors about the program. Students also get a chance to interact with college students and find out what literacy skills are most important for a successful college experience.

38. How should teachers best instruct students in writing?

    a. In connection with reading only
    b. By itself to focus student attention
    c. With relation to reading and speaking
    d. Related to listening, reading, and speaking

39. A teacher has a child who does not volunteer in class. When the teacher asks the student a question the student can answer, she does so with as few words as possible. The teacher isn't sure how to best help the child. She should:

a. Leave the child alone. She is clearly very shy and will be embarrassed by having attention drawn to her. She is learning in her own way.

b. Ask two or three highly social children to include this girl in their activities. She is shy, and she probably won't approach them on her own.

c. Observe the child over the course of a week or two. Draw her into conversation and determine if her vocabulary is limited, if she displays emotional problems, or if her reticence could have another cause. Note how the child interacts with others in the class. Does she ever initiate conversation? If another child initiates, does she respond?

d. Refer her to the school counselor immediately. It is clear the child is suffering from either a low IQ or serious problems at home.

40. The source of the silent *b* in the English word *debt* was originally...

a. A Middle English word.
b. A voiced Old English *b.*
c. From Latin etymology.
d. The Greek etymology.

41. Which choice describes the most complete method of displaying student achievement or progress in language arts?

a. A written report or story that demonstrates a student's knowledge of grammar, spelling, comprehension, and writing skills.

b. Either a norm- or criterion-referenced test that breaks language skills into small subsets and provides achievement levels for each skill.

c. A portfolio containing a log of stories or books the student has read, rates of reading fluency, writing samples, creative projects, and spelling, grammar, and comprehension tests/quizzes.

d. A year-end project in which the student presents what he or she has learned from a student-chosen book; the student must read an excerpt of the story and display a visual aid highlighting important information from the story or literary techniques used by the author.

42. Among four categories of media that teachers instruct students to identify, in which one are books primarily classified?

a. Media used in one-on-one communication
b. Media used for entertainment
c. Media to inform many people
d. Media for persuading people

43. A sixth-grade student is able to decode most words fluently and has a borderline/acceptable vocabulary, but his reading comprehension is quite low. He can be helped with instructional focus on:

a. Strategies to increase comprehension and to build vocabulary
b. Strategies to increase comprehension and to be able to identify correct syntactical usage
c. Strategies to improve his understanding of both content and context
d. Strategies to build vocabulary and to improve his understanding of both content and context

44. The questions in this test can give you an idea of what kinds of questions you might find on the actual test; however, they are not duplicates of the actual test questions, which cover the same knowledge but may differ somewhat in form and content.

The preceding sentence is which of the following sentence types?

    a. Simple
    b. Complex
    c. Compound
    d. Compound-complex

45. Which assessment will determine a student's ability to identify initial, medial, blended, final, segmented, and manipulated 'units'?

    a. Phonological awareness assessment
    b. High-frequency word assessment
    c. Reading fluency assessment
    d. Comprehension quick-check

46. A student identifies a text to read independently. According to an informal reading inventory the teacher just conducted, the student understands 48 percent of words in isolation that this text includes; reads words contained in this text with 90 percent accuracy in context; and correctly answers 68 percent of comprehension questions at this text's reading level. What does this indicate to the teacher?

    a. This text is at the student's independent level; the teacher approves the student's selection.
    b. This text is at the student's frustration level; the teacher helps the student find another text.
    c. This text is at the student's instructional level, and the teacher approves it for guided reading.
    d. This text is at some reading level that cannot be identified only from the student information.

47. Which of the following choices represents the smallest unit of language that possesses semantic meaning?

    a. Morpheme
    b. Grapheme
    c. Phoneme
    d. Word stem

48. Which of the following expressions is equivalent to $-3x(x-2)^2$?

    a. $-3x^3 + 6x^2 - 12x$
    b. $-3x^3 - 12x^2 + 12x$
    c. $-3x^2 + 6x$
    d. $-3x^3 + 12x^2 - 12x$

49. McKenzie shades $\frac{1}{5}$ of a piece of paper. Then, she shades an additional area $\frac{1}{5}$ the size of what she just shaded. Next, she shades another area $\frac{1}{5}$ as large as the previous one. As she continues the process to infinity, what is the limit of the shaded fraction of the paper?

    a. $\frac{1}{5}$
    b. $\frac{1}{4}$
    c. $\frac{1}{3}$
    d. $\frac{1}{2}$

50. Which of the following represents the net of a triangular prism?

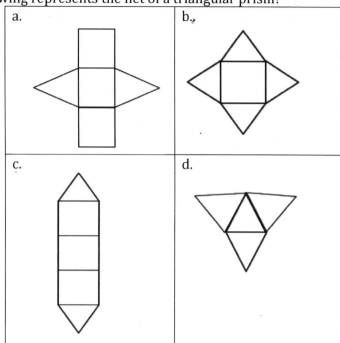

a.

b.

c.

d.

51. Andrew rolls a die. What is the probability he gets a 4 or an even number?

a. $\frac{1}{4}$

b. $\frac{1}{2}$

c. $\frac{2}{3}$

d. $\frac{3}{4}$

52. Which of the following learning goals is most appropriate for a second grade unit on personal financial literacy?

a. The students will be able to calculate how money saved can accumulate into a larger amount over time.

b. The students will be able to balance a simple budget.

c. The students will be able to identify the costs and benefits of planned and unplanned spending decisions.

d. The students will be able to define money earned as income.

53. Which of the following options represents equivalency between different representations of rational numbers?

a. $16 \div (6 - 4)^2 = 64$

b. $8 - 2(7 - 4) = 18$

c. $2^3 \div 2 - 2(2) = 0$

d. $2 + 3(2^2) = 20$

54. Claus has $20 to spend at the local fun fair. The entrance fee is $2.50 and tickets for the booths are $2 each. Which of the following inequalities represents the number of tickets Claus can afford with his $20?

    a. $2.50x + 2x \leq 20$
    b. $2.50 + 2x \leq 20$
    c. $2x \leq 20 + 2.50$
    d. $2.50 + 2x \geq 20x$

55. A teacher is assessing the students' understanding of the appropriate units for length, area, and volume. Which of the following only lists units of area?

    a. in², mm², ft²
    b. yd, yd2, yd3
    c. mm, cm, m
    d. m², s², km²

56. Ms. Elliott asks her 5th-grade students, "Do you prefer chocolate or vanilla ice cream?" If the probability of her students preferring chocolate ice cream is 0.6, what is the probability of her students preferring vanilla ice cream?

    a. 0.6
    b. 0.4
    c. 0.3
    d. 0.5

57. While teaching the concept of addition, a first-grade teacher gives each student two dice to use as manipulatives. Which of the following types of representation is this teacher using to communicate this concept?

    a. Concrete
    b. Verbal
    c. Graphic
    d. Pictorial

58. The variables x and y are in a linear relationship. The table below shows a few sample values. Which of the following graphs correctly represents the linear equation relating x and y?

x	y
−2	−11
−1	−8
0	−5
1	−2
2	1

a.

b.

c.

d.

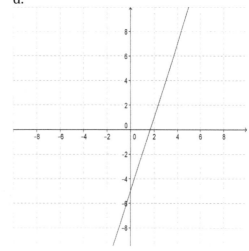

59. What is the midpoint of the line segment below?

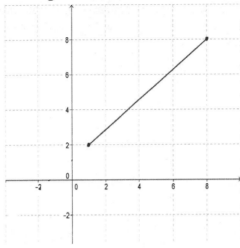

    a. $(3.5, 4)$
    b. $(4, 4)$
    c. $(4.5, 5)$
    d. $(5, 5)$

60. Ann must walk from Point A to Point B and then to Point C. Finally, she will walk back to Point A. If each unit represents 5 miles, which of the following best represents the total distance she will have walked?

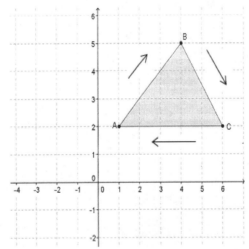

    a. 42 miles
    b. 48 miles
    c. 56 miles
    d. 64 miles

61. When planning a unit on linear equations, a teacher would most likely include discussion on which of the following topics?
    a. Conjugating to remove irrational denominators
    b. Gradient of a straight line
    c. Order of operations
    d. Characteristics of the diagonals of various quadrilaterals

62. Two companies offer monthly cell phone plans, both of which include free text messaging. Company A charges a $25 monthly fee plus five cents per minute of phone conversation, while Company B charges a $50 monthly fee and offers unlimited calling. Both companies charge the same amount when the total duration of monthly calls is

    a. 500 hours.
    b. 8 hours and 33 minutes.
    c. 8 hours and 20 minutes.
    d. 5 hours.

63. Solve the system of equations.
$$3x + 4y = 2$$
$$2x + 6y = -2$$

    a. $\left(0, \frac{1}{2}\right)$
    b. $\left(\frac{2}{5}, \frac{1}{5}\right)$
    c. $(2, -1)$
    d. $\left(-1, \frac{5}{4}\right)$

64. Identify the cross-section polygon formed by a plane containing the given points on the cube.

    a. Rectangle
    b. Trapezoid
    c. Pentagon
    d. Hexagon

65. In order to analyze the real estate market for two different zip codes within the city, a realtor examines the most recent 100 home sales in each zip code. She considered a house which sold within the first month of its listing to have a market time of one month; likewise, she considered a house to have a market time of two months if it sold after having been on the market for one month but by the end of the second month. Using this definition of market time, she determined the frequency of sales by number of months on the market. The results are displayed below.

Which of the following is a true statement for these data?

a. The median time a house spends on the market in Zip Code 1 is five months less than Zip Code 2

b. On average, a house spent seven months longer on the market in Zip Code 2 than in Zip Code 1.

c. The mode time on the market is higher for Zip Code 1 than for Zip Code 2.

d. The median time on the market is less than the mean time on the market for Zip Code 1.

66. Jason decides to donate 1% of his annual salary to a local charity. If his annual salary is $45,000, how much will he donate?

a. $4.50

b. $45

c. $450

d. $4,500

67. Kevin saves $3 during Month 1. During each subsequent month, he plans to save 4 more dollars than he saved during the previous month. Which of the following equations represents the amount he will save during the nth month?

a. $a_n = 3n - 1$

b. $a_n = 3n + 4$

c. $a_n = 4n + 3$

d. $a_n = 4n - 1$

68. A tree with a height of 15 feet casts a shadow that is 5 feet in length. A man standing at the base of the shadow formed by the tree is 6 feet tall. How long is the shadow cast by the man?

    a. 1.5 feet
    b. 2 feet
    c. 2.5 feet
    d. 3 feet

69. The simulation of a coin toss is completed 300 times. Which of the following best represents the number of tosses you can expect to show heads?

    a. 50
    b. 100
    c. 150
    d. 200

70. Mr. Mancelli teaches fifth-grade math. He is making prize bags for the winners of a math game. If he has eight candy bars and twelve packages of gum, what is the largest number of identical prize bags he can make without having any left-over candy bars or packages of gum?

    a. 2
    b. 4
    c. 6
    d. 8

71. Which of the following goals is appropriate in the category of algebraic reasoning for first-grade students?

    a. Students represent one- and two-step problems involving addition and subtraction of whole numbers to 1,000 using pictorial models, number lines, and equations.
    b. Students represent real-world relationships using number pairs in a table and verbal descriptions.
    c. Students represent word problems involving addition and subtraction of whole numbers up to 20 using concrete and pictorial models and number sentences.
    d. Students recite numbers up to at least 100 by ones and tens beginning with any given number.

72. Which of the following descriptions best fits a hexagonal prism?

    a. 8 faces, 18 edges, 12 vertices
    b. 6 faces, 18 edges, 12 vertices
    c. 8 faces, 16 edges, 8 vertices
    d. 6 faces, 14 edges, 10 vertices

73. Addison tosses a six-sided die twelve times and records the results in the table below.

Toss	1	2	3	4	5	6	7	8	9	10	11	12
Results	2	5	1	2	3	6	6	2	4	5	4	3

Which of the following statements is true?

    a. The experimental probability of tossing a 6 is greater than the theoretical probability.
    b. The experimental probability of tossing a 3 is greater than the theoretical probability.
    c. The experimental probability of tossing a 1 is greater than the theoretical probability.
    d. The experimental probability of tossing a 2 is greater than the theoretical probability.

74. If $f(x) = \frac{x^3 - 2x + 1}{3x}$, what is $f(2)$?

   a. $\frac{1}{3}$

   b. $\frac{1}{2}$

   c. $\frac{5}{6}$

   d. $\frac{5}{2}$

75. What is the distance on a coordinate plane from $(-8, 6)$ to $(4, 3)$?

   a. $\sqrt{139}$
   b. $\sqrt{147}$
   c. $\sqrt{153}$
   d. $\sqrt{161}$

76. $A = \{9, 4, -3, 8, 6, 0\}$ and $B = \{-4, 2, 8, 9, 0\}$. What is $A \cup B$?

   a. $\{9, 8, 0\}$
   b. $\{9, 4, -3, 8, 6, 0, -4, 2\}$
   c. $\emptyset$
   d. $\{9, 8, 0, 2, 4\}$

77. On a floor plan drawn at a scale of 1:100, the area of a rectangular room is 30 cm^2. What is the actual area of the room?

   a. 30,000 cm^2
   b. 3,000 cm^2
   c. 3,000 m^2
   d. 30 m^2

78. A developer decides to build a fence around a neighborhood park, which is positioned on a rectangular lot. Rather than fencing along the lot line, he fences x feet from each of the lot's boundaries. By fencing a rectangular space 141 yd^2 smaller than the lot, the developer saves $432 in fencing materials, which cost $12 per linear foot. How much does he spend?

   a. $160
   b. $456
   c. $3,168
   d. The answer cannot be determined from the given information.

79. Which of the following statements is true of the data?

   a. The mean better reflects student performance in class 1 than the median.
   b. The mean test score for class 1 and 2 is the same.
   c. The median test score for class 1 and 2 is the same.
   d. The median test score is above the mean for class 4.

80. A circular bracelet contains 5 charms, A, B, C, D, and E, attached at specific points around the bracelet, with the clasp located between charms A and B. The bracelet is unclasped and stretched out into a straight line. On the resulting linear bracelet, charm C is between charms A and B, charm D is between charms A and C, and charm E is between charms C and D. Which of these statements is (are) necessarily true?

> I. The distance between charms B and E is greater than the distance between charms A and D.
> II. Charm E is between charms B and D.
> III. The distance between charms D and E is less than the distance of bracelet between charms A and C.

    a. I, II, and III
    b. II and III
    c. II only
    d. None of these is necessarily true.

81. A gift box has a length of 14 inches, a height of 8 inches, and a width of 6 inches. How many square inches of wrapping paper are needed to wrap the box?

    a. 56
    b. 244
    c. 488
    d. 672

82. Eli rolls a die and tosses a coin. What is the probability he gets a prime number or tails?

    a. $\frac{1}{4}$
    b. $\frac{1}{3}$
    c. $\frac{1}{2}$
    d. $\frac{3}{4}$

83. Ms. Chen is instructing her students on divisibility rules. Which of the following rules can be used to determine if a number is divisible by 6?

    a. The last digit of the number is divisible by 2 or 3.
    b. The number ends in 6.
    c. The number is divisible by 2 and 3.
    d. The last two digits of the number are divisible by 6.

84. Marcus, a sixth-grade student, is mowing yards and doing odd jobs to earn money for a new video game system that costs $325. Marcus only charges $6.50 per hour. Which of the following equations represents the number of hours Marcus needs to work to earn $325?

    a. $6.50x = 325$
    b. $6.50 + x = 325$
    c. $325x = 6.50$
    d. $6.50x + 325 = x$

85. Which of the following best describes the significance of the U.S. Supreme Court's decision in the Dred Scott case?

    a. The ruling effectively declared slavery to be a violation of the Constitution.
    b. The ruling guaranteed full citizenship rights to freed slaves.
    c. The ruling turned many Southerners against the Supreme Court.
    d. The ruling furthered the gap between North and South and hastened the Civil War.

86. The Tropic of Capricorn:

    a. separates the northern and southern hemispheres.
    b. separates the eastern and western hemispheres.
    c. is the southernmost latitude at which the sun can appear directly overhead at noon.
    d. is the northernmost latitude at which the sun can appear directly overhead at noon.

87. The Seven Years War, called the French and Indian War by the Colonists:

    a. Was the precursor to the American Revolution
    b. Was a conflict related to European colonization
    c. Primarily took place in Canada
    d. Ended European conquests

88. Which of the following statements is *not* an accurate statement about the Puritans in England?

    a. The Puritans unconditionally gave all their support to the English Reformation
    b. The Puritans saw the Church of England as too much like the Catholic Church
    c. The Puritans became a chief political power because of the English Civil War
    d. The Puritans' clergy mainly departed from the Church of England after 1662

89. Which part of a hurricane features the strongest winds and greatest rainfall?

    a. Eye wall
    b. Front
    c. Eye
    d. Outward spiral

90. Most federal judges have served as local judges, lawyers, and law professors. These are _____ qualifications.

    a. Formal
    b. Required
    c. Informal
    d. Recommended

91. Which of the following were dispatch riders notifying Americans of British troop movements reported by American surveillance in 1775?

    a. Paul Revere and John Parker
    b. William Dawes and Paul Revere
    c. Andrew Johnson and William Dawes
    d. John Parker and Phillip Dumay

92. The physical geography of a region most directly affects:
    a. The religious beliefs of the native population.
    b. The family structure of the native population.
    c. The dietary preferences of the native population.
    d. The language spoken by the native population

93. The price of oil drops dramatically, saving soda pop manufacturers great amounts of money spent on making soda pop and delivering their product to market. Prices for soda pop, however, stay the same. This is an example of what?
    a. Sticky prices
    b. Sticky wages
    c. The multiplier effect
    d. Aggregate expenditure

94. What does the 10th Amendment establish?
    a. Any power not given to the federal government belongs to the states or the people
    b. The President is responsible for executing and enforcing laws created by Congress
    c. Congress has the authority to declare war
    d. The Supreme Court has the authority to interpret the Constitution

95. The Mason-Dixon Line divided:
    a. The East from the West before the western states were incorporated
    b. The East from the West along the Mississippi River
    c. The North from the South before the Civil War
    d. The Senate from the House of Representatives

96. The philosophy of the late 17th-18th centuries that influenced the Constitution was from the Age of:
    a. Enlightenment
    b. Empire
    c. Discovery
    d. Industry

97. Which geographic features were most conducive to the development of early civilizations?
    a. Rivers
    b. Deserts
    c. Forests
    d. Mountains

98. What portion of the federal budget is dedicated to transportation, education, national resources, the environment, and international affairs?
    a. Mandatory spending
    b. Discretionary spending
    c. Undistributed offsetting receipts
    d. Official budget outlays

99. Thomas Jefferson embraced a theological philosophy called deism, which promotes which of the following?

a. Abolition
b. Atheism
c. Separation of church and state
d. A theocratic central government

100. When the Senate held an impeachment hearing against Andrew Johnson for overstepping his authority, what did they invoke?

a. Checks and balances
b. Bicameralism
c. Judicial intervention
d. Supremacy

101. The first ten amendments to the Constitution are more commonly known as:

a. The Civil Rights Act
b. Common law
c. The Equal Protection clause
d. The Bill of Rights

102. A country's currency increases in value on foreign currency exchange markets. What will happen as a result?

I. Exports will drop
II. Imports will rise
III. The balance of payments will rise

a. I only
b. II only
c. I and II
d. II and III

103. Which statement about factors related to the growth of the US economy between 1945 and 1970 is incorrect?

a. The Baby Boom's greatly increased birth rates contributed to economic growth during this time.
b. The reduction in military spending after World War II contributed to the stronger US economy.
c. Government programs and growing affluence nearly quadrupled college enrollments in 20 years.
d. Increased mobility and bigger families caused fast suburban expansion, especially in the Sunbelt.

104. The civil rights act that outlawed segregation in schools and public places also:

a. Gave minorities the right to vote
b. Established women's right to vote
c. Outlawed unequal voter registration
d. Provided protection for children

105. Which of the following world religions is the oldest?

    a. Greek Stoicism
    b. Confucianism
    c. Christianity
    d. Judaism

106. Which of the following is associated with market failure?

    I. When a firm in a non-competitive industry hires labor at a lower wage
    II. When the firms in a non-competitive industry create less than the efficient amount of a good or service
    III. When production of a good creates negative externalities born by third parties
    IV. Public goods

    a. I and II only
    b. I and III only
    c. I, II, and III only
    d. I, II, III, and IV

107. Which of the following statements is incorrect regarding these religions under the Roman Empire?

    a. The Romans generally protected the Jews until the rebellion in Judea (66 C.E.)
    b. Julius Caesar circumvented Roman law to help Jews have freedom of worship
    c. The Druids were a religious group that the Romans ignored but also tolerated
    d. Romans viewed Christianity as a Jewish sect for its first two centuries

108. A major cause of the Great Depression of the 1930s was:

    a. the overproduction and underconsumption of consumer goods.
    b. the failure of industry to produce sufficient consumer goods.
    c. underproduction and rising prices in the agricultural sector.
    d. the reduction of import tariffs.

109. The concept of checks and balances is evident in which of the following?

    a. Federal judiciary appeals
    b. Presidential veto
    c. States' rights
    d. The House and the Senate

110. What is the most common type of volcano on earth?

    a. Lava dome
    b. Composite volcano
    c. Shield volcano
    d. Cinder cone

111. Of the following statements, which is true about the March on Versailles during the French Revolution?

    a. The March on Versailles was an action undertaken by equal numbers of both men and women
    b. The March on Versailles was an action undertaken primarily by women
    c. The March on Versailles happened prior to the storming of the Bastille
    d. The March on Versailles was not effective in accomplishing its purpose

112. What judicial system did America borrow from England?

　a. Due process
　b. Federal law
　c. Commerce law
　d. Common law

113. The precedent for the two-term limit for the US Presidency was established by:

　a. Abraham Lincoln
　b. Alexander Hamilton
　c. George Washington
　d. Thomas Jefferson

114. How are animals of the Mollusca phylum able to respire?

　a. Through gills
　b. Through a trachea
　c. Through lungs
　d. Through muscle contraction

115. A pulley lifts a 10 kg object 10 m into the air in 5 minutes. Using this information, you can calculate:

　a. mechanical advantage
　b. efficiency
　c. energy conservation
　d. power

116. Two companion models, gradualism and punctuated equilibrium, dominate evolutionary theory. Which of the following statements is MOST consistent with the theory of punctuated equilibrium?

　a. Fossils show changes over large periods of time.
　b. Fossils showing intermediate characteristics may not necessarily be found.
　c. Speciation occurs gradually.
　d. Evolution is a slow, steady process.

117. How are igneous rocks formed?

　a. Years of sediment are laid down on top of each other and forced together
　b. Acid rain caused by pollution creates holes in metamorphic rocks
　c. Dust and pebbles are pressed together underground from Earth's heat and pressure
　d. Magma from a volcanic eruption cools and hardens

118. The following represents a simple food chain. What trophic level contains the greatest amount of energy?

　　Tree -> Caterpillar -> Frog -> Snake -> Hawk -> Worm

　a. Tree
　b. Caterpillar
　c. Hawk
　d. Worm

119. What happens to gas particles as temperature increases?

a. The average kinetic energy decreases while the intermolecular forces increase.
b. The average kinetic energy increases while the intermolecular forces decrease.
c. Both the average kinetic energy and the intermolecular forces decrease.
d. Both the average kinetic energy and the intermolecular forces increase.

120. Which of the following represents a chemical change?

a. Sublimation of water
b. A spoiling apple
c. Dissolution of salt in water
d. Pulverized rock

121. What type of compound is formed by the combination of two or more non-metallic elements with one another?

a. Organic
b. Ionic
c. Covalent
d. Chemical

122. Which of the following is an example of chemical weathering?

a. Rain freezing on the roadway
b. Ivy growing on the side of a wooden house
c. Vinegar fizzing when poured on a rock
d. A river carrying sediment downstream

123. Which of the following is an example of a descriptive study?

a. correlational studies of populations
b. identifying a control
c. statistical data analysis
d. identifying dependent and independent variables

124. What happens to the temperature of a substance as it is changing phase from a liquid to a solid?

a. Its temperature increases due to the absorption of latent heat.
b. Its temperature decreases due to the heat of vaporization.
c. Its temperature decreases due to the latent heat of fusion.
d. Its temperature remains the same due to the latent heat of fusion.

125. Which of the following is never true of a chemical reaction?

a. Matter is neither gained nor lost.
b. Heat is absorbed or released.
c. The rate of the reaction increases with temperature.
d. There are a different number of atoms for the products and the reactants.

126. Fossils are least likely to be found in

a. sedimentary rock.
b. metamorphic rock.
c. igneous rock.
d. Fossils are commonly found in all types of rock.

127. Which of the following statements correctly describes a similarity or difference between rocks and minerals?

    a. Minerals may contain traces of organic compounds, while rocks do not.
    b. Rocks are classified by their formation and the minerals they contain, while minerals are classified by their chemical composition and physical properties.
    c. Both rocks and minerals can be polymorphs.
    d. Both rocks and minerals may contain mineraloids.

128. Which of the following is true of an isotope?

    a. It has a different number of protons than its element.
    b. It has a different number of electrons than its element.
    c. It has a different charge as compared to its element.
    d. It has a different number of neutrons than its element.

129. Which action will help dissolve a gas in a liquid if the gas and liquid are placed in a sealed container?

    a. Heat the liquid.
    b. Cool the liquid.
    c. Shake the container.
    d. Decrease the pressure on the lid.

130. Compared to fresh water, the freezing point of sea water is

    a. higher.
    b. lower.
    c. the same.
    d. Sea water does not freeze.

131. Tropical climate zones are characterized by:

    a. Extreme temperature variations between night and day.
    b. Extreme temperature variations between seasons.
    c. Frequent rainfall.
    d. Relatively constant, cold temperatures (35°F - 45°F)

132. The process whereby a radioactive element releases energy slowly over a long period of time to lower its energy and become more stable is best described as _____.

    a. combustion
    b. fission
    c. fusion
    d. decay

133. This organelle contains digestive enzymes that break down food and unneeded substances. They are also thought to be linked to the aging process. What part of a cell does this describe?

    a. Lysosomes
    b. Chromatin
    c. Plastids
    d. Golgi Apparatus

134. On a topographic map, an area where the contour lines are very close together indicates that
    a. a stream is present.
    b. the slope is very gentle.
    c. the slope is very steep.
    d. the area surrounds a depression.

135. The distance from the Earth to the Sun is equal to one:
    a. Astronomical unit.
    b. Lightyear.
    c. Parsec.
    d. Arcsecond.

136. Which of the following observations provides the best evidence that sound can travel through solid objects?
    a. Sound waves cannot travel through a vacuum.
    b. The atoms of a solid are packed tightly together.
    c. If you knock on a solid object, it makes a sound.
    d. You can hear a sound on the other side of a solid wall.

137. Which division of plants produces seeds for reproduction?
    a. Anthophyta
    b. Lycophyta
    c. Sphenophyta
    d. Pterophyta

138. Which of the following creates a magnetic field?
    a. the spinning and rotating of electrons in atoms
    b. the separation of charged particles in atoms
    c. the vibrational and translational motion of atoms
    d. loosely held valence electrons surrounding an atom

139. The asteroid belt in our solar system is located between:
    a. Earth and Mars.
    b. Neptune and Pluto.
    c. Uranus and Saturn.
    d. Mars and Jupiter.

140. In a parallel circuit, there are three paths: A, B and C. Path A has a resistance of 10 ohms, path B a resistance of 5 ohms and part C a resistance of 2 ohms. How do the voltage and current change for each path?
    a. Voltage and current are kept the same in each path.
    b. Voltage is greatest in path A and current is greatest in path C.
    c. Voltage is lowest in path C and current is greatest in path C.
    d. Voltage is the same for each path and current is greatest in path C.

Answer Key and Explanations

1. B: Researchers have found that the writing processes both form a hierarchy and are observably recursive in nature. Moreover, they find that when students continually revise their writing, they are able to consider new ideas and to incorporate these ideas into their work. Thus, they do not merely correct mechanical errors when revising (A), they also add to the content and quality of their writing. Furthermore, research shows that writers, including students, not only revise their actual writing; during rewrites, they also reconsider their original writing goals rather than always retaining them (C), and they revisit their prewriting plans rather than leaving these unaffected in rewriting (D).

2. C: Once the students' notecards have been checked and edited for accuracy, they can easily be used to demonstrate the process of organizing ideas in an essay or research paper. Students can use their notecards as aids for making their outlines. They simply have to arrange the notecards in an appropriate order and add pertinent information to bridge the ideas together in their writing.

3. D: Rate, accuracy, and prosody. Fluent readers are able to read smoothly and comfortably at a steady pace (rate). The more quickly a child reads, the greater the chance of leaving out a word or substituting one word for another (for example, *sink* instead of *shrink*). Fluent readers are able to maintain accuracy without sacrificing rate. Fluent readers also stress important words in a text, group words into rhythmic phrases, and read with intonation (prosody).

4. C: Are homophones. Homophones are words that are pronounced the same but differ in meaning. For example, a bride wears a 2 caret ring, but a horse eats a carrot.

5. A: It is a standard of Information Literacy (IL) that students must use their own critical thinking skills to evaluate the quality of the information and its sources before they use it. Another standard is that the student should ascertain how much information s/he needs for his/her purposes first; deciding this after uncovering excessive information is inefficient (B). An additional IL standard is to access necessary information in an efficient and effective way. However, none of these standards include the idea that students will lose incidental learning or broadness of scope by doing so (C). IL standards include the principle that students *should* use the information they find in ways that are effective for attaining their specific purposes (D).

6. B: Spelling is often taught in a systematic way. Students receive words and memorize them for quizzes and tests. However, spelling is related to many aspects of language and must be treated as a dynamic subject. Integrating the words into other parts of language instruction will help students not only learn how to spell correctly, but also to recall meanings of words and various rules of English spelling and grammar. By using the same words in different subjects, the students will retain the information more readily than if they study the words intensely for one week in only one context.

7. C: Tier-two words. Tier-two words are words that are used with high frequency across a variety of disciplines or words with multiple meanings. They are characteristic of mature language users. Knowing these words is crucial to attaining an acceptable level of reading comprehension and communication skills.

8. D: Teachers will observe a variety of developmental arcs when teaching reading since all students learn differently. It is very important to understand which instances are normal in the course of learning and which signal a learning difficulty. Barrett is still exhibiting confusion over

74

certain letter-sounds, typically when the letters look similar. At his age, this difficulty could suggest that Barrett has an issue with reading that could be addressed by a reading specialist. The other three choices describe normal behaviors that are commonly exhibited by children when they are learning to read. Choice C, Noelle, may describe an instance in which a student is having a learning problem. However, the teacher will need more information about Noelle's reading skills besides her reluctance to read before making a determination about how to proceed.

9. D: The MLA guidelines for citing multiple authors of the same work in in-text citations (for both print and online sources) dictate using the first author's name plus "et al" for the other authors when there are four or more authors. If there are two (options A and B) or three (options B and C) authors, the guidelines say to name each author, either in a signal phrase [for example, "Smith and Jones note that... (45)" or "Smith, Jones, and Gray have noted... (45)"] or in a parenthetical reference ["(Smith, Jones, and Gray 45)."].

10. A: The /p/ sound is among the earliest phonemes to develop, from ages 1.5 to 3 years old. The /ʒ/ phoneme (B) has the oldest age norm for normal development—5.5 years to 8.5 years old is a typical range for children to acquire correct production of this sound. The /v/ sound (C) typically develops in most children from the ages of 4 to 8 years. Most children develop correct articulation of the /s/ sound (D) by 2.5 to 4 years old. Hence, not all kindergarteners, who are typically around 5 years old, are expected to master phonemes with acquisition norm ranges older than 5-8 years. A 5-year-old is *most* likely to be referred for SLP evaluation if s/he does not correctly produce /p/, which children normally develop by around 3 years old.

11. B: Prior knowledge is knowledge the student brings from previous life or learning experiences to the act of reading. It is not possible for a student to fully comprehend new knowledge without first integrating it with prior knowledge. Prior knowledge, which rises from experience and previous learning, provides a framework by which new knowledge gained from the act of reading can be integrated. Every act of reading enriches a student's well of prior knowledge and increases that student's future ability to comprehend more fully any new knowledge acquired through reading.

12. B: Vocabulary. The tightly controlled syllabic requirements will cause students to search for words outside their normal vocabularies that will fit the rigid framework and still express the writer's intended meanings. Often, students will rediscover a word whose meaning they know, but they don't often use.

13. A: Mnemonic devices are a way to aid in memorization. The concept to be memorized is linked to a device: an easily remembered song, saying, or image. To remember the concept, one needs only to remember the device.

14. A: While there is no consensus among experts as to any universal sequence of instruction for teaching the alphabetic principle through phonics instruction, they do agree that, to enable children to start reading words as soon as possible, the highest-utility relationships should be introduced earliest. For example, the letters *m, a, p, t,* and *s* are all used frequently, whereas the *x* in *box*, the sound of *ey* in *they*, and the letter *a* when pronounced as it is in *want* have lower-utility letter-sound correspondences. Important considerations for the alphabetic principle are to teach letter-sound correspondences in isolation, not in word contexts (B); to teach them explicitly; to give students opportunities to practice letter-sound relationships within their other daily lessons, not only separately (C); and to include cumulative reviews of relationships taught earlier along with new ones in practice opportunities (D).

15. A: Letter–sound correspondence. Letter–sound correspondence relies on the relationship between a spoken sound or group of sounds and the letters conventionally used in English to write them.

16. A: Clarifying the goal, modeling strategies, and offering explanations geared to a student's level of understanding. Explicit instruction is well organized and structured, and it offers easily understood steps and depends in part on frequent reference to previously learned materials.

17. C: Diction refers to your overall choice of language for your writing, while vocabulary refers to the specific words in a discipline that you use when writing in or about that discipline—not vice versa (A). Jargon (B) is very specialized terminology used in a discipline that is not readily understood by readers outside of that discipline. It is hence less accessible than the vocabulary of the discipline and only used in writing intended only for those who are already familiar with it. Diction and vocabulary are elements of writing style (D).

18. B: Students must be able to distinguish between printed words and the spaces between them to identify the first and last letters of each word, as spaces are the boundaries between words. It is not true that all normally developing students can tell words from spaces (A): those not exposed to or familiar with print media may need to be taught this distinction. Although left-to-right directionality is more of a problem for ELL students whose L1s have different writing or printing directions (e.g., some Asian languages are written vertically, some can be written vertically or horizontally, and some Semitic languages like Hebrew and Arabic are written right-to-left), again, children unfamiliar with print or writing may also not know writing, print, or book directionality either (C). Identifying basic punctuation is important to reading comprehension as it affects meaning. For example, consider "Let's eat, Grandma" vs. "Let's eat Grandma"—one comma differentiates an invitation to dinner from a cannibalistic proposal.

19. A: Fewer than 50 words in the time given. At the beginning of the school year, second-grade students should be able to read 50–80 words per minute. By the time they are well into the school year, second-grade-level reading is tracked at 85 words per minute.

20. A: Avoid idioms and slang, involve students in hands-on activities, reference students' prior knowledge, and speak slowly. Teachers of English Language Learners should not employ idioms and slang in their instruction because these informal uses of speech are likely to confuse the students. Involving students in hands-on activities such as group reading and language play makes the experience both more meaningful and more immediate. New knowledge can only be absorbed by attaching it to prior knowledge, referencing what students already know is essential. Speaking slowly to English Language Learners is important because they are processing what is being said at a slower rate than a native speaker.

21. A: Evaluation is the most complex of the thinking/writing strategies listed in these choices because it commonly incorporates the other thinking strategies. Knowledge recall (D) requires showing mastery of information learned. Comprehension (C) requires showing understanding of the information learned. Application (B) requires taking the information learned and using it in new or different circumstances. These processes are not as complex as evaluating (or making critical judgments) the information learned. Analysis, synthesis, and evaluation are more complex than knowledge recall, comprehension, and application. Of analysis, synthesis, and evaluation, evaluation is the most complex.

22. D: To instruct students in word analysis following a sequence progressing from simpler to more complex, teachers would first introduce individual phonemes (speech sounds); then the blending of two or more individual phonemes; then onsets and rimes, i.e., phonograms and word families (e.g., -ack, -ide, -ay, -ight, -ine, etc.); then the easier short vowels, followed by the more difficult long vowels; then blends of individual consonants; then CVC (consonant-vowel-consonant) words (e.g., *bag, hot, red, sit,* etc.) and other common patterns of consonants and vowels in words; and then the six most common types of syllables (closed, VCe, open, vowel team, r-controlled, and C-le).

23. C: Students can easily become bored or disinterested in reading if they are not exposed to a variety of reading texts. Also, reading can be overwhelming or frustrating for students who are still learning to read fluently or to comprehend what they read. By incorporating media, oral stories, and various types of print, students of all ability levels can build both fluency and comprehension skills. This approach also enables the teacher and students to discuss the relationship between all aspects of literacy, including speaking, listening, thinking, viewing, and reading.

24. B: Phonemic awareness. Vocalizing words involves arranging a series of continuous, voiced, unvoiced, and stop sounds. As one sound is being uttered, the tongue and lips are already assuming the shape required by the next sound in the word. This process, which is not conscious, can distort individual sounds. One sound can slur into another, clip the end of the previous sound, or flatten or heighten a sound. For children who have difficulty hearing distinct phonemic sounds, individual instruction may be required.

25. B: This prompt focuses not only on reading fluency skills but also on the issue of the young reader's confidence. It is very common for students who feel unsuccessful at reading to avoid the skill altogether. The teacher in this question realizes something important: it is vital to build a student's confidence with reading as he or she builds skill. In choice A there is a faulty assumption that a student could ever memorize enough words to eliminate the need to decode. While some students with processing disorders or different learning styles do rely more heavily on sight words, this practice should not be solely relied upon. In choice C the students will likely feel negative about being asked to read young children's books; their lack of confidence may be reinforced by this plan. In choice D students may also be frustrated by the extra work they are required to do without any evidence of success with this practice. In Choice B, students can build their fluency skills by creating words with various sounds, which is often easier for students than decoding as they are learning to read. As their knowledge of letter-sound relationships grows, they will become better at decoding words they see on the page. Allowing students to encode will also provide them with more chances to feel successful as they learn.

26. B: Identifying point of view (A) is an example of *literal* reading comprehension. Explaining the point of view (B) is an example of *evaluative* reading comprehension. Identifying the main idea of a text passage (C) is an example of *literal* reading comprehension. Making predictions about what will happen in a text (D) is an example of *inferential* reading comprehension.

27. C: Cause–effect words. Signal words give the reader hints about the purpose of a particular passage. Some signal words are concerned with comparing/contrasting, some with cause and effect, some with temporal sequencing, some with physical location, and some with a problem and its solution. The words *since, whether,* and *accordingly* are words used when describing an outcome. Outcomes have causes.

28. C: The Syntactic Cueing System is that set of cues available in the syntax. Syntax is the sentence structure and word order of language. The Phonological (A) Cueing System is that set of cues available in the phonological structure of language. Phonological structure is the language's speech sounds and the letters representing them. The Semantic (B) Cueing System is that set of cues available in the semantics. Semantics are the meaning (and meanings) of words and the morphemes (smallest units of meaning) that comprise words. The Three Cueing Systems model does not include a Pragmatic (C) system. However, it recognizes, as all linguists and reading instructors do, that pragmatic cues involve reader understanding of their reasons for reading and of how text structures operate. (In linguistics, pragmatics is the study of how language is used for social communication.)

29. B: There are many different adults who can assist children in acquiring various types of language. If a child inconsistently mispronounces certain sounds in reading, he or she may simply need a reminder or instruction from a teacher. Often, children will not acquire knowledge of certain letters or sounds until a certain age. However, the child in this scenario mispronounces words consistently both in reading and in conversation. This combination suggests that the child is not physically able to make certain speech sounds. A speech-language pathologist can assist in determining whether or not the child's mispronunciations indicate the need for therapy. This type of therapist can also work directly with the child to help him or her learn how to make certain sounds.

30. B: Indirect ways in which students receive instruction and learn vocabulary include through daily conversations, reading on their own, and being read aloud to by adults. Direct instruction and learning in vocabulary include teachers' providing extended instruction exposing students repeatedly to vocabulary words in multiple teaching contexts (A), teachers' pre-teaching specific words found in text prior to students' reading it (C), and teachers' instructing students over extended time periods (D) and having them actively work with vocabulary words.

31. C: Identify and use groups of letters that occur in a word family. Analogizing is based on recognizing the pattern of letters in words that share sound similarities. If the pattern is found at the end of a family of words, it is called a *rhyme*. Some examples of rhyme are *rent, sent, bent,* and *dent.* If the pattern is found at the beginning of the family of words, it is frequently a consonant *blend* such as *street, stripe,* or *strong,* in which all the letters are pronounced, or the pattern is a consonant digraph, in which the letters are taken together to represent a single sound such as in *phone, phonics,* or *phantom.*

32. A: The student making this observation is connecting reading of a mythological text (presumably Greek or Roman) s/he reads to the world—in this instance, to human nature—by noting that despite greater powers, the gods' emotional reactions and behaviors are like those of humans. The student statement in choice B reflects a connection of text to text—fiction (a novel) to historical accounts of a period (for example, see Dickens's *A Tale of Two Cities).* The student statement in option C reflects a connection of text to self: the student can relate to the feelings of a character in the text. Because each choice reflects a different one of the three kinds of student connections named, choice D is incorrect.

33. B: Reading responses can take various forms. The most common form of reading response is likely to be targeted student writing. Students may use journals, worksheets, or other formats to construct written responses to something they have read. The purpose of this type of assignment can range from fostering an appreciation of written text to helping a student prepare for an activity in class. Students may also engage in creating an oral reading response in the form of a presentation or debate. Ultimately, reading response increases a student's capacity to understand what he or she has read and to analyze personal responses to the text.

34. C: Depending on their type, graphs can be used to compare quantities or values at the same point in time (or irrespective of time), or to show changes in quantities or values over time. For example, a bar graph can show different numbers of students in different categories, different test scores, etc. next to each other for comparison, or different numbers yearly, monthly, weekly, daily, etc. Line graphs only show changes in values over time. Tables (A) are good for organizing information into categories but do not show linear changes over time. Maps (B), when cartographic (actual maps), depict geographical locations and can include other information (e.g., population totals, percentages, income, domestic or national product figures, annual rainfall, temperatures, etc.) via color-coding and other graphics. Other map types used in education, including concept maps for students, curriculum maps and resource maps for educators, etc. do not show linear chronological change. Charts (D), e.g., pie charts, which show percentages or proportions of a whole quantity divided by categories, do not show change over time.

35. C: Context. By considering the other words in the story, the student can determine the missing words. The student is depending on the information supplied by the rest of the story. This information puts the story into context.

36. C: L2s can be learned in a number of educational contexts, such as being segregated from the L1, formally taught via the medium of the L1, through submersion, or within the language classroom but not used to communicate outside it, among many others. They can also be taught/learned in several natural contexts: as the majority language to members of ethnic minority groups, as the official language of a country where learners speak a different language, or for international communication purposes separate from the L1 or official language. Therefore, it is not accurate that L2s are never learned in natural contexts (B and D). Unlike L2s, L1s are always first acquired in natural contexts, meaning choice A is inaccurate.

37. B: In this project, students will engage in almost every aspect of literacy in a group context. Students must first accurately read and comprehend a short play; they will also use their writing skills to adapt the play to their specific purposes by cutting or adding text. The teacher can gauge the students' interpretive skills by the way they perform their play. By splitting the students into groups, the teacher can provide each student the chance to interpret and perform, as well as to experience the performances. Audience members receive additional practice with listening and interpreting when they generate responses to the performances. Group members can evaluate the effectiveness of their performances based on responses from the audience.

38. D: Teachers should instruct students in writing not in isolation (B), not relating writing only to reading (A) or reading and speaking (C), but by showing students the interrelationships of listening, speaking, reading, and writing. In addition, teachers should not just teach writing as a rote chore or drill, but give students lessons and assignments that demonstrate legitimate purposes for writing and provide topics to write about that are meaningful to students.

39. C: Observe the child over the course of a week or two. Draw her into conversation and determine if her vocabulary is limited, if she displays emotional problems, or if her reticence could have another cause. Note how the child interacts with others in the class. Does she ever initiate conversation? If another child initiates, does she respond? Until the teacher monitors the child's verbal abilities and habits, she cannot determine if the lack of interaction suggests a learning disability, an emotional problem, or simply a shy personality. The teacher should informally observe the child over a period of time, noting if and when she initiates or responds to oral language, if she is reading with apparent comprehension, if her vocabulary is limited, and the degree to which the child is interested in understanding.

40. C: The etymology, or origin, of the English word *debt*, is the Latin word *debitum*. It came into English during the Middle English form of the language. Therefore, this word was not originally a Middle English word (A) but a Latin word. Because it came from Latin into Middle English, it did not exist as an Old English word with a voiced *b* (B) as Old English preceded Middle English. The origin of this word was not Greek (D) but Latin. NOTE: Early scribes and printers, described by some as "inkhorn scholars," introduced many silent letters to English spellings to indicate their Latin or Greek roots, as in this case.

41. C: Literacy skills are various and include a number of different sub-skills: reading fluency, comprehension, application of knowledge, listening, speaking, grammar, spelling, writing, and more. It is important for teachers to track student development for lesson design and to communicate with the student, future teachers, and parents. Therefore, it is best to keep samples of a variety of assessments, including descriptions of reading fluency, writing samples, projects, and formal assessments of grammar, spelling, and other skills. All of these skills develop simultaneously, but at different rates. Therefore, it is impossible to judge a student's literacy based only on one measure of assessment.

42. C: When teaching students about various media types, the four categories listed as choices are ways to classify them. Option A includes emails, phone calls, and letters but not books. Option B includes movies, TV shows, video games; and novels are included, but not the wider class of books. (Note that there are many more kinds of books than novels.) Option C includes books, newspapers, websites, and radio news broadcasts. Option D includes advertising, direct mail marketing, telemarketing calls, and infomercials.

43. A: Strategies to increase comprehension and to build vocabulary. The student should receive instruction focused on just those areas in which he is exhibiting difficulty. Improved vocabulary will give him greater skill at comprehending the meaning of a particular text. Strategies focused on enhancing comprehension together with a stronger vocabulary will provide the greatest help.

44. D: This is an example of a compound-complex sentence. A simple (A) sentence contains a subject and a verb and expresses a complete thought. Its subject and/or verb may be compound (e.g., "John and Mary" as subject and "comes and goes" as verb). A complex (B) sentence contains an independent clause and one or more dependent clauses. The independent and dependent clause(s) are joined by a subordinating conjunction or a relative pronoun. A compound (C) sentence contains two independent clauses—two simple sentences—connected by a coordinating conjunction. A compound-complex (also called complex-compound) sentence, as its name implies, combines both compound and complex sentences: it combines more than one independent clause with at least one dependent clause. In the example sentence given, the first two clauses, joined by "however," are independent, and the clause modifying "actual test questions," beginning with "which cover," is a relative, dependent clause.

45. A: The words in this question prompt are most often used to refer to *sounds* made while reading. Initial/onset, medial, and final sounds are decoded in the beginning, middle, and end of words. When a teacher needs to assess an emergent or struggling reader's ability to differentiate between sounds in words, he or she may use a phonological awareness assessment. This tool will provide the teacher with information about the student's current ability to decode or encode words.

46. B: One set of criteria suggested for use with informal reading inventories (Pumfrey, 1976) equates the independent reading level (A) to knowing 95-100 percent of words in isolation, 99-100 percent accuracy reading words in context, and answering comprehension questions 90-100 percent correctly; the instructional level (C) to knowing 60-94 percent of words in isolation, 95-98 percent accuracy reading words in context, and answering comprehension questions 70-89 percent correctly; and the frustration level with knowing below 50 percent of words in isolation, reading below 95 percent of words accurately in context, and answering below 70 percent of comprehension questions correctly. Hence, the text described is at the student's frustration level and too difficult. Because the student information identifies reading levels below these suggested criteria for the frustration level, choice D is incorrect.

47. A: A phoneme is a unit of language that represents the smallest unit of sound. For instance, the *k* in "kit" or the *ph* in "graph" both represent English phonemes. Graphemes are written phonemes and can be alphabetic letters, numbers, characters, punctuation marks, and so on. Neither phonemes nor graphemes have semantic meaning unless they are used as part of a larger unit of language, such as the morpheme. Morphemes can be roots, prefixes, and suffixes. The word "rechargeable" is comprised of three morphemes: "re," "charge," and "able." Each component of this word has a meaning unto itself, but when combined with the others, each one is used to make a new word with a new meaning.

48. D: The expression $(x - 2)^2$ may be expanded as $x^2 - 4x + 4$. Multiplication of $-3x$ by this expression gives $-3x^3 + 12x^2 - 12x$.

49. B: The sequence $\frac{1}{5}, \frac{1}{25}, \frac{1}{125}, \frac{1}{625}, \ldots$, may be used to represent the situation. Substituting the initial value of $\frac{1}{5}$ and common ratio of $\frac{1}{5}$ into the formula $S = \frac{a}{1-r}$ gives $= \frac{\frac{1}{5}}{1-\frac{1}{5}}$, which simplifies to $S = \frac{\frac{1}{5}}{\frac{4}{5}}$ or $S = \frac{1}{4}$.

50. A: The net of a triangular prism has three rectangular faces and two triangular faces. This is true of both choices A and C, but choice C cannot be folded into a triangular prism because the two rectangular faces on the end cannot be made to join each other. So only choice A can be folded into a triangular prism.

51. B: Since they are not mutually exclusive events, the probability may be written as $P(4 \text{ or } E) = P(4) + P(E) - P(4 \text{ and } E)$. Substituting the probability of each event gives $(4 \text{ or } E) = \frac{1}{6} + \frac{1}{2} - \frac{1}{6}$, or $\frac{1}{2}$.

52. A: Choice A is correct because the standards for second-grade state that students will be able to calculate how money saved can accumulate into a larger amount over time. Choice D, which is included in the standards for first grade, is too basic for second grade. Choice C is stated in the standards for third grade. Choice B is stated in the fifth grade standards. Therefore, the correct choice is A.

53. C: Only choice C correctly applies the order of operations. The left side of choice A is equivalent to 4. The left side of choice B is equivalent to 2. The left side of choice D is equivalent to 14. Therefore, the correct choice is C.

54. B: Since Claus has at most $20 to spend, the amount he spends must be less than or equal to ($\leq$) $20, which eliminates choice D. Since the entrance fee of $2.50 is only charged once, it should not be multiplied by x, so choice A is also incorrect. The cost of the entrance fee ($2.50) and the cost of the tickets ($2x$) should be added together to find the Claus's total cost of the fun fair. This eliminates choice C. The correct inequality is $2.50 + 2x \leq 20$. Therefore, the correct choice is B.

55. A: Since area is two dimensional, the units for area have an exponent of two such as in², yd², cm², or m². Choice B includes a unit of length (yd) and a unit of volume (yd³). Choice C includes only units of length. Choice C includes a square unit of time (s²). Therefore, the correct choice is A.

81

Copyright © Mometrix Media. You have been licensed one copy of this document for personal use only. Any other reproduction or redistribution is strictly prohibited. All rights reserved.

56. B: Since the events are mutually exclusive, the sum of their individual probabilities is 1.0. Subtracting 0.6 from 1.0 yields 0.4. Therefore, the correct choice is B.

57. A: The teacher is using a concrete representation of the concept in question, since the dice she is using are a physical object which help communicate the concept. Verbal, graphic, and pictorial are not correct since the student is not merely observing a discussion about the concept or even graphic representation. Concrete representations often lead to more depth of knowledge and better retention of the concepts.

58. D: The table shows the y-intercept to be −5. The slope is equal to the ratio of change in y-values to change in corresponding x-values. As each x-value increases by 1, each y-value increases by 3. Thus, the slope is $\frac{3}{1}$, or 3. This graph represents the equation $y = 3x - 5$.

59. C: The midpoint may be calculated by using the formula $m = \left(\frac{x_1+x_2}{2}, \frac{y_1+y_2}{2}\right)$. Thus, the midpoint of the line segment shown may be written as $m = \left(\frac{1+8}{2}, \frac{2+8}{2}\right)$, which simplifies to $m = (4.5, 5)$.

60. D: The perimeter of the triangle is equal to the sum of the side lengths. The length of the longer diagonal side may be represented as $d = \sqrt{(4-1)^2 + (5-2)^2}$, which simplifies to $d = \sqrt{18}$. The length of the shorter diagonal side may be represented as $d = \sqrt{(6-4)^2 + (2-5)^2}$, which simplifies to $d = \sqrt{13}$. The base length is 5 units. Thus, the perimeter is equal to $5 + \sqrt{18} + \sqrt{13}$, which is approximately 12.85 units. Since each unit represents 5 miles, the total distance she will have walked is equal to the product of 12.85 and 5, or approximately 64 miles.

61. B: The gradient of a straight line refers to the slope of the line. This concept is vital to understanding linear equations. Choices A and C may be introduced during similar studies. However, *all* linear equations will involve gradients. Choice D suggests that quadrilaterals may be related to linear equations; however, the two concepts are not directly related.

62. C: The expression representing the monthly charge for Company A is $\$25 + \$0.05m$, where m is the time in minutes spent talking on the phone. Set this expression equal to the monthly charge for Company B, which is $50. Solve for m to find the number of minutes for which the two companies charge the same amount:

$$\$25 + \$0.05m = \$50$$
$$\$0.05m = \$25$$
$$m = 500$$

Notice that the answer choices are given in hours, not in minutes. Since there are 60 minutes in an hour, $m = \frac{500}{60}$ hours $= 8\frac{1}{3}$ hours. One-third of an hour is twenty minutes, so $m = 8$ hours, 20 minutes.

63. C: A system of linear equations can be solved by using matrices or by using the graphing, substitution, or elimination (also called linear combination) method. The elimination method is shown here:

$$3x + 4y = 2$$
$$2x + 6y = -2$$

In order to eliminate x by linear combination, multiply the top equation by 2 and the bottom equation by −3 so that the coefficients of the x-terms will be additive inverses.

$$2(3x + 4y = 2)$$
$$-3(2x + 6y = -2)$$

Then, add the two equations and solve for y.

$$6x + 8y = 4$$
$$\underline{-6x - 18y = 6}$$
$$-10y = 10$$
$$y = -1$$

Substitute -1 for y in either of the given equations and solve for x.

$$3x + 4(-1) = 2$$
$$3x - 4 = 2$$
$$3x = 6$$
$$x = 2$$

The solution to the system of equations is $(2, -1)$.

64. D: The cross-section is a hexagon.

65 D:

Time on market	Frequency for Zip Code 1	Frequency for Zip Code 2	Time Frequency for Zip Code 1	Time Frequency for Zip Code 1
1	9	6	9	6
2	10	4	20	8
3	12	3	36	9
4	8	4	32	16
5	6	3	30	15
6	5	5	30	30
7	8	2	56	14
8	8	1	64	8
9	6	3	54	27
10	3	5	30	50
11	5	7	55	77
12	4	6	48	72
13	2	6	26	78
14	3	5	42	70
15	1	3	15	45
16	2	2	32	32
17	2	3	34	51
18	1	5	18	90
19	0	6	0	114
20	2	4	40	80
21	1	5	21	105
22	1	4	22	88
23	0	3	0	69
24	1	5	24	120
SUM	100	100	738	1274

Since there are 100 homes' market times represented in each set, the median time a home spends on the market is between the 50th and 51st data point in each set. The 50th and 51st data points for Zip Code 1 are six months and seven months, respectively, so the median time a house in Zip Code 1 spends on the market is between six and seven months (6.5 months), which by the realtor's definition of market time is a seven-month market time. The 50th and 51st data points for Zip Code 2 are both thirteen months, so the median time a house in Zip Code 2 spends on the market is thirteen months.

To find the mean market time for 100 houses, find the sum of the market times and divide by 100. If the frequency of a one-month market time is 9, the number 1 is added nine times (1·9), if the frequency of a two-month market time is 10, the number 2 is added ten times (2·10), and so on. So, to find the average market time, divide by 100 the sum of the products of each market time and its corresponding frequency. For Zip Code 1, the mean market time is 7.38 months, which by the realtor's definition of market time is an eight-month market time. For Zip Code 2, the mean market time is 12.74, which by the realtor's definition of market time is a thirteen-month market time.

The mode market time is the market time for which the frequency is the highest. For Zip Code 1, the mode market time is three months, and for Zip Code 2, the mode market time is eleven months.

The statement given in choice D is true. The median time a house spends on the market in Zip Code 1 is less than the mean time a house spends on the market in Zip Code 1.

66. C: The amount he donates is equal to 0.01(45,000). Thus, he donates $450.

67. D: This situation may be modeled by an arithmetic sequence, with a common difference of 4 and an initial value of 3. Substituting the common difference and initial value into the formula, $a_n = a_1 + (n - 1)d$, gives $a_n = 3 + (n - 1)4$, which simplifies to $a_n = 4n - 1$.

68. B: The following proportion may be written and solved for x: $\frac{15}{5} = \frac{6}{x}$. Solving for x gives $x = 2$. Thus, the shadow cast by the man is 2 feet in length.

69. C: The theoretical probability is $\frac{1}{2}$, and $\frac{1}{2}(300) = 150$.

70. B: Since Mr. Mancelli has eight candy bars, he can make at most eight identical bags, each containing a single candy bar and a single package of gum; in this case, however, he will have four packages of gum remaining. To determine the greatest number of prize bags he can make so that no candy bars or packages of gum remain, he needs to find the greatest common divisor (or greatest common factor) of 8 and 12. Factors of 8 include 1, 2, 4, and 8. Factors of 12 include 1, 2, 3, 4, 6, and 12. The greatest common divisor of 8 and 12 is 4. He can make four prize bags, each of which contains two candy bars and three packages of gum. Therefore, the correct choice is B.

71. C: Only choice C is the appropriate level for first-grade students. Choices A and B are appropriate for third-grade students. Choice D is appropriate for kindergarten. Therefore, the correct choice is C.

72. A: A hexagon has six ides. A hexagonal prism has 8 faces consisting of two hexagonal bases and six rectangular lateral faces. This results in 18 edges and 12 vertices. Therefore, the correct choice is A.

73. D: The theoretical probability of tossing any particular number is $\frac{1}{6}$. Since she tosses a two $\frac{3}{12}$, or $\frac{1}{4}$, times, the experimental probability of tossing a 2 is greater than the theoretical probability. The experimental probability should grow closer to the experimental probability as she tosses the die more times. Therefore, the correct choice is D.

74. C: Substituting 2 for each x-value gives $f(2) = \frac{2^3 - 2(2) + 1}{3(2)}$, which simplifies to $f(2) = \frac{5}{6}$.

75. C: The distance may be calculated using the distance formula, $d = \sqrt{(x_2 - x_1)^2 + (y_2 - y_1)^2}$. Substituting the given coordinates, the following equation may be written: $d = \sqrt{(4 - (-8))^2 + (3 - 6)^2}$, which simplifies to $d = \sqrt{153}$.

76. B: $A \cup B$ means "A union B," or all of the elements in either of the two sets. "A union B" represents "A or B," that is, an element is in the union of A and B if it is in A *or* it is in B. The elements in sets A and B are 9, 4, −3, 8, 6, 0, −4, and 2.

77. D: Since there are 100 cm in a meter, on a 1:100 scale drawing, each centimeter represents one meter. Therefore, an area of one square centimeter on the drawing represents one square meter in actuality. Since the area of the room in the scale drawing is 30 cm², the room's actual area is 30 m².

Another way to determine the area of the room is to write and solve an equation, such as this one:

$\frac{l}{100} \cdot \frac{w}{100} = 30$ cm² , where l and w are the dimensions of the actual room

$$\frac{lw}{1000} = 30 \text{ cm}^2$$
$$lw = 300{,}000 \text{ cm}^2$$
$$\text{Area} = 300{,}000 \text{ cm}^2$$

Since this is not one of the answer choices, convert cm² to m²: $300{,}000 \text{ cm}^2 \cdot \frac{1 \text{ m}}{100 \text{ cm}} \cdot \frac{1 \text{ m}}{100 \text{ cm}} = 30 \text{ m}^2$.

78. C: If l and w represent the length and width of the enclosed area, its perimeter is equal to $2l + 2w$; since the fence is positioned x feet from the lot's edges on each side, the perimeter of the lot is $2(l + 2x) + 2(w + 2x)$. Since the amount of money saved by fencing the smaller are is $432, and since the fencing material costs $12 per linear foot, 36 fewer feet of material are used to fence around the playground than would have been used to fence around the lot. This can be expressed as the equation $2(l + 2x) + 2(w + 2x) - (2l + 2w) = 36$.

$$2(l + 2x) + 2(w + 2x) - (2l + 2w) = 36$$
$$2l + 4x + 2w + 4x - 2l - 2w = 36$$
$$8x = 36$$
$$x = 4.5 \text{ ft}$$

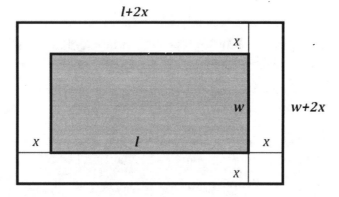

The difference in the area of the lot and the enclosed space is 141 yd², which is the same as 1269 ft². So, $(l + 2x)(w + 2x) - lw = 1269$. Substituting 4.5 for x,

$$(l + 9)(w + 9) - lw = 1269$$
$$lw + 9l + 9w + 81 - lw = 1269$$
$$9l + 9w = 1188$$
$$9(l + w) = 1188$$
$$l + w = 132 \text{ ft}$$

Therefore, the perimeter of the enclosed space, $2(l + w)$, is $2(132) = 264$ ft. The cost of 264 ft of fencing is $264 \cdot \$12 = \$3{,}168$.

79. C: The line through the center of the box represents the median. The median test score for classes 1 and 2 is 82.

80. B: The problem does not give any information about the size of the bracelet or the spacing between any of the charms. Nevertheless, creating a simple illustration which shows the order of the charms will help when approaching this problem. For example, the circle below represents the bracelet, and the dotted line between A and B represents the clasp. On the right, the line shows the stretched out bracelet and possible positions of charms C, D, and E based on the parameters.

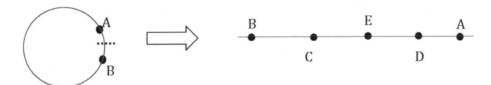

From the drawing above, it appears that statement I is true, but it is not necessarily so. The alternative drawing below also shows the charms ordered correctly, but the distance between B and E is now less than that between D and A.

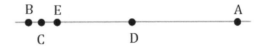

Statement II must be true: charm E must lie between B and D. Statement III must also be true: the distance between charms E and D must be less than that between C and A, which includes charms E and D in the space between them.

81. C: The surface area of a rectangular prism may be calculated using the formula $SA = 2lw + 2wh + 2hl$. Substituting the dimensions of 14 inches, 6 inches, and 8 inches gives $SA = 2(14)(6) + 2(6)(8) + 2(8)(14)$. Thus, the surface area is 488 square inches.

82. D: Since they are not mutually exclusive events, the probability may be written as $P(P \text{ or } T) = P(P) + P(T) - P(P \text{ and } T)$. Because the events are independent, $P(P \text{ and } T) = P(P) \cdot P(T)$. Substituting the probability of each event gives $(P \text{ or } T) = \frac{1}{2} + \frac{1}{2} - \left(\frac{1}{2} \cdot \frac{1}{2}\right)$, or 1.

83. C: A number that is divisible by 6 is divisible by 2 and 3. For example, the number 12 is divisible by 2 and 3. A number ending in 6, a number with the last two digits divisible by 6 and a number with the last digit divisible by 2 or 3 is not necessarily divisible by 6; for example, 16 and 166 are not divisible by 6. Therefore, the correct choice is C.

84. A: Marcus needs $325 for the new gaming system. If he earns $6.50 an hour, the number of hours he needs to work can be determined by dividing $325 by $6.50 which is written as $\frac{325}{6.50} = x$. Multiplying both sides of the equation by 6.50 yields $6.50x = 325$. Therefore, the correct choice is A.

85. D: In the Dred Scott decision of 1857, the Court ruled that no slave or descendant of slaves could ever be a United States citizen. It also declared the Missouri Compromise of 1820 to be unconstitutional, clearing the way for the expansion of slavery in new American territories. This ruling pleased Southerners and outraged the North further dividing the nation and setting the stage for war.

86. C: Lying at a little more than 23° south of the equator, the Tropic of Capricorn is the border between the Southern Temperate Zone to the south and the Tropical Zone to the north. The southern hemisphere is tilted toward the sun to its maximum extent each year at the winter solstice in December. The northernmost latitude at which the sun can appear directly overhead is at the Tropic of Cancer during the summer solstice. The northern and southern hemispheres are separated by the equator at 0° degrees latitude. The eastern and western hemispheres are separated by the prime meridian at 0° longitude.

87. B: The Seven Years War was a global military conflict. In the Americas, the conflict was largely between Western European countries, Great Britain and France, in particular.

88. A: The inaccurate statement is the Puritans unconditionally supported the English Reformation. While they agreed with the Reformation in principle, they felt that it had not pursued those principles far enough and should make greater reforms. Similarly, they felt that the Church of England (or Anglican Church), though it had separated from the Catholic Church in the Protestant Reformation, still allowed many practices they found too much like Catholicism (B). The Puritans did become a chief political power in England because of the first English Civil War (C) between Royalists and Parliamentarians. The Royalists had a profound suspicion of the radical Puritans. Among the Parliament's elements of resistance, the strongest was that of the Puritans. They joined in the battle initially for ostensibly political reasons as others had, but soon they brought more attention to religious issues. Following the Restoration in 1660 and the Uniformity Act of 1662, thereby restoring the Church of England to its pre-English Civil War status, the great majority of Puritan clergy defected from the Church of England (D). It is also accurate that the Puritans in England disagreed about separating from the Church of England. Some Puritans desired complete separation; they were known first as Separatists and after the Restoration as Dissenters. Others did not want complete separation but instead desired further reform in the Church of England. While they remained part of the Church of England, they were called Non-Separating Puritans, and after the Restoration, they were called Nonconformists.

89. A: The eye wall of a hurricane has the strongest winds and the greatest rainfall. The eye wall is the tower-like rim of the eye. It is from this wall that clouds extend out, which are seen from above as the classic outward spiral pattern. A hurricane front is the outermost edge of its influence; although there will be heavy winds and rain in this area, the intensity will be relatively small. The eye of a hurricane is actually a place of surprising peace. In this area, dry and cool air rushes down to the ground or sea. Once there, the air is caught up in the winds of the eye wall and is driven outward at a furious pace.

90. C: There are no formal qualifications for members of the judicial branch. However, having a background in law is an informal qualification that is considered when appointing Article III judges.

91. B: Paul Revere and William Dawes were both dispatch riders who set out on horseback from Massachusetts to spread news of British troop movements across the American countryside around the beginning of the War of Independence. John Parker was the captain of the Minutemen militia, who were waiting for the British at Lexington, Massachusetts.

92. C: Physical geography focuses on processes and patterns in the natural environment. What people eat in any given geographic region is largely dependent on such environmental factors as climate and the availability of arable land. Religion, family, and language may all be affected by geographical factors, but they are not as immediately affected as dietary preferences.

93. A: The phenomenon of "sticky prices" refers to prices that stay the same even though it seems they should change (either increasing or decreasing).

94. A: The 10th Amendment establishes that any power not given to the federal government in the Constitution belongs to the states or the people. The federal and local governments share many responsibilities.

95. C: The Mason-Dixon Line was the manifestation of a border dispute between Great Britain and the colonists. It effectively separated, or illustrated, a cultural divide between North and South before the Civil War.

96. A: The Age of Enlightenment was a time of scientific and philosophical achievement. Also called the Age of Reason, it was a time when human thought and reason were prized.

97. A: Rivers promoted the development of the ancient river valley civilizations of the world, including in the Middle East, India, and China. Rivers not only supply water for drinking and crop irrigation; they also provide fertile soil, vegetation for shade cover, food, building materials, and animal life. They additionally allow water travel to other locations. Although some peoples have settled and lived in deserts, they are among the most inhospitable climates. Forests also provide plenty of flora and fauna and exist in areas receiving enough rainfall, but rivers have been historically superior in attracting human societies. Mountains near living areas provide protective barriers; however, though some peoples live there, as in deserts, living in the mountains is difficult due to high altitudes, harsh climates, poor soil for planting, and rough terrain.

98. B: Discretionary spending is dedicated to transportation, education, national resources, the environment, and international affairs. State and local governments use this money to help finance programs. Mandatory spending covers entitlements such as Medicare, Social Security, Federal Retirement, and Medicaid.

99. C: Thomas Jefferson embraced John Locke's concept of separation of church and state. Deism posits that a Supernatural force created the world and universe, but that He did not intervene after creation. Jefferson wanted minimal central governing, just as he viewed the Creator's relationship with the universe.

100. A: Checks and balances were established to keep one branch of government from taking too much authority. When Johnson violated the Tenure of Office Act by replacing Secretary of War Edwin Stanton, Johnson was impeached, but the final vote in the Senate trial came up one vote short of the number needed to convict him.

101. D: The Bill of Rights was drafted by Congress to limit the authority of the government and protect the rights of individual citizens from abuse by the federal government. It was the first document to detail the rights of private citizens.

102. C: If a country's currency increases in value, foreigners will have to give up more of their own currency to get the original country's currency in order to buy the original country's goods and services. This will cause a drop-in exports. At the same time, it will be less expensive for people in the original country to exchange their currency for foreign currencies, causing the price of imported goods to drop and the total value of imports to rise.

103. B: There was not a reduction in military spending after the war. Although the manufacturing demand for war supplies and the size of the military decreased, the government had increased military spending from $10 billion in 1947 to more than $50 billion by 1953—a more than fivefold increase. This increase strengthened the American economy. Other factors contributing to the strengthened economy included the significantly higher birth rates during the Baby Boom (A) from 1946 to 1957, which stimulated the growth of the building and automotive industries by increased demand. Government programs, such as the GI Bill (the Servicemen's Readjustment Act of 1944), other veterans' benefits, and the National Defense Education Act all encouraged college enrollments, which increased by nearly four times (C). Additionally, larger families, increased mobility and low-interest loans offered to veterans led to suburban development and growth (D) as well as an increased home construction. Improvements in public health were also results of the new affluence; the rate of infant deaths decreased significantly, and as a result, from 1946-1957, the American life span rose from 67 to 71 years. Moreover, Dr. Jonas Salk developed the polio vaccine in 1955, which virtually wiped out poliomyelitis, preventing many deaths and disabilities in children.

104. C: The Civil Rights Act of 1964 affected the Jim Crowe laws in the Southern states. Many minorities suffered under unfair voting laws and segregation. President Lyndon Johnson signed the Civil Rights Act of 1964 into law after the 1963 assassination of President Kennedy, who championed the reform.

105. D: Judaism has existed since around 1300 B.C.E. according to historians' estimates. The Greek religion of Stoicism was founded by Zeno in Athens around 313 B.C.E., almost 1,000 years later than Judaism. Confucianism was founded in China by Confucius, who lived from 551 to 479 B.C.E., around 800 years after Judaism. Christianity dates to approximately 30 C.E. in Israel.

106. D: A market failure is any situation in which the production of a good or service is not efficient. In the cases listed, non-competitive markets allow for the underpayment of labor and the underproduction of a good or service; externalities are negative consequences assumed by parties not involved in a transaction; and public goods are an example of a good the market will not produce at all, or at efficient levels.

107. C: The Druids were neither ignored nor tolerated by the Romans. Conversely, the Druids were viewed as "non-Roman" and therefore were suppressed. Augustus (63 B.C.E.-14 C.E.) forbade Romans to practice Druid rites. According to Pliny, the Senate under Tiberius (42 B.C.E.-37 C.E.) issued a decree suppressing Druids, and in 54 C.E., Claudius outlawed Druid rites entirely. It is correct that the Romans generally protected the Jews up until the rebellion in Judea in 66 C.E. (A). In fact, Julius Caesar circumvented the Roman laws against "secret societies" by designating Jewish synagogues as "colleges," which in essence permitted Jews to have freedom of worship (B). After the rebellion in Judea, according to Suetonius, the Emperor Claudius appeared to have expelled all Jews, probably including early Christians, from Rome. The Roman Empire viewed Christianity as a Jewish sect, which was how Christianity began, for 200 years following its emergence (D). It is also correct that according to Tacitus, when much of the public saw Emperor Nero as responsible for the Great Fire of Rome in 64 C.E. (the origin of the old saying "Nero fiddled while Rome burned"), Nero blamed the Christians for the fire in order to deflect guilt from himself. Following their persecution of Jews, the Roman Empire would continue to persecute Christians for the next two centuries.

108. A: Along with stock market speculation, a major cause of the Great Depression was an increased supply of cars, radios, and other goods that was not matched by consumer demand. Industrial production far exceeded the population's purchasing power. Farmers were plagued by overproduction and falling prices while international trade suffered from rising tariffs.

109. B: The President may veto legislation passed by Congress. The executive branch has this "check" on the legislative branch.

110. B: The composite volcano, sometimes called the stratovolcano, is the most common type of volcano on earth. A composite volcano has steep sides, so the explosions of ash, pumice, and silica are often accompanied by treacherous mudslides. Indeed, it is these mudslides that cause most of the damage associated with composite volcano eruptions. Krakatoa and Mount Saint Helens are examples of composite volcanoes. A lava dome is a round volcano that emits thick lava very slowly. A shield volcano, one example of which is Mt. Kilauea in Hawaii, emits a small amount of lava over an extended period of time. Shield volcanoes are not known for violent eruptions. A cinder cone has steep sides made of fallen cinders, which themselves are made of the lava that intermittently shoots into the air.

111. B: The only true statement is the March on Versailles was made primarily by women. Therefore, an equal number of both men and women did not undertake the March on Versailles (A). The women took action because of the dire economic conditions from which they suffered, especially the high prices on bread and food shortages. The storming of the Bastille occurred on July 14, 1789; the March on Versailles occurred on October 5, 1789, almost three months later, not prior to it (C). (The date of July 14th is so famous as Bastille Day in France that generally it is familiar in other countries as well.) It is not true that the March on Versailles was not effective in accomplishing its purpose (D). In fact, the marchers did achieve their goal: They stormed the palace and killed several guards. La Fayette, in charge of the National Guard to control the mob, convinced the royals to move from Versailles to Paris and to stop blocking the National Assembly, and the royal family complied with these demands. The women did not march right to Versailles without preliminaries. First, they assembled in markets around Paris and marched to the Hôtel de Ville. There they made their demands of the Paris city officials. When those officials did not give acceptable responses, the women then joined a march to the palace at Versailles. While the march to Versailles included men and weapons, some 7,000 women made up the majority of the marchers.

112. D: America is a common law country because English common law was adopted in all states except Louisiana. Common law is based on precedent and changes over time. Each state develops its own common laws.

113. C: George Washington served 2 four-year terms as President. This interval of time was not specified in the Constitution, but future Presidents followed suit (until FDR).

114. A: Through gills. Animals of the phylum Mollusca respire through gills. Respiration is the process of taking in oxygen and releasing carbon dioxide. Mollusks include five classes that include species as diverse as chitons, land and marine snails, and squid. This represents a diverse range of body structures. Many mollusks have a mantle that includes a cavity that is used for both breathing and excretion. Within the mantle are gills (ctenidia). Mollusks do not have tracheas. Some land snails have reduced gills that feature a respiratory cavity but are not true lungs. Muscle contraction is not required for ventilation of the gills. Other structures, such as cilia, work to pass water over the gills.

115. D: Power = work / time. The mass of the object (10 kg) and the distance (10 m) can be used to calculate work. The value for time is also provided.

116. B: Gradualism states that evolution occurs slowly, with organisms exhibiting small changes over long periods of time. According to gradualism, the fossil record should show gradual changes over time. Punctuated equilibrium states that evolution occurs in spurts of sudden change. According to punctuated equilibrium, the fossil record should have large gaps. Therefore, the correct answer is choice B.

117. D: Igneous rocks are formed when magma in Earth erupts through cracks in the crust where it cools creating a hard structure with many air pockets or holes.

118. A: Tree. In the food chain of Tree -> Caterpillar -> Frog -> Snake -> Hawk -> Worm, the tree is at the trophic level with the greatest amount of energy. Trophic level refers to the position of an organism in a food chain. Energy is lost according to the laws of thermodynamics as one moves up the food chain because it is converted to heat when consumers consume. Primary producers, such as autotrophs, are organisms who are at the base and capture solar energy. Primary consumers are herbivores that feed on the producers. Secondary consumers consume primary consumers and so on. Decomposers get their energy from the consumption of dead plants and animals.

119. B: Temperature is a measure of the kinetic energy of particles. As temperature increases the average kinetic energy also increases. As the gas particles move more rapidly they occupy a larger volume. The increase in speed of the individual particles combined with the greater distance over which any intermolecular forces must act results in a decrease in the intermolecular forces.

120. B: A spoiling apple. A spoiling apple is an example of a chemical change. During a chemical change, one substance is changed into another. Oxidation, a chemical change, occurs when an apple spoils. Sublimation of water refers to the conversion between the solid and the gaseous phases of matter, with no intermediate liquid stage. This is a phase change, not a chemical reaction. Dissolution of salt in water refers to a physical change since the salt and water can be separated again by evaporating the water, which is a physical change. Pulverized rock is an example of a physical change where the form has changed but not the substance itself.

121. C: Covalent. Covalent compounds are usually formed by the combination of two or more non-metallic elements with one another. In these compounds atoms share electrons. Ionic compounds are most often formed between a metal and a non-metal. Organic compounds are covalent compounds which contain carbon and hydrogen atoms. "Chemical compounds" is a general term that can mean any type of compound, either ionic or covalent.

122. C: Vinegar fizzing when poured on a rock is an example of chemical weathering. Mechanical and chemical weathering are processes that break down rocks. Mechanical weathering breaks down rocks physically but does not change their chemical composition. Frost and abrasion are examples. Water, oxygen, carbon dioxide and living organisms can lead to the chemical weathering of rock. Vinegar is a weak acid and will undergo a chemical reaction, evidenced by fizzing, with the rock. Rain freezing on the roadway is an example of the phase change of water from a liquid to a solid and may lead to physical weathering. Ivy growing on the side of a wooden house is incorrect since the house is not a rock. A river carrying sediment downstream is an example of erosion.

123. A: A correlational study of a population is an example of a descriptive study. Choices B and C are examples of the controlled experimentation type of scientific investigation. Choice D is an example of the comparative data analysis type of scientific investigation.

124. D: Its temperature remains the same due to the latent heat of fusion. The temperature of a substance during the time of any phase change remains the same. In this case, the phase change was from liquid to solid, or freezing. Latent heat of fusion, in this case, is energy that is released from the substance as it reforms its solid form. This energy will be released and the liquid will turn to solid before the temperature of the substance will decrease further. If the substance were changing from solid to liquid, the heat of fusion would be the amount of heat required to break apart the attractions between the molecules in the solid form to change to the liquid form. The latent heat of fusion is exactly the same quantity of energy for a substance for either melting or freezing.

Depending on the process, this amount of heat would either be absorbed by the substance (melting) or released (freezing).

125. D: There may be a different number of atoms for the products and the reactants. This is not true of a chemical reaction. Chemical equations must be balanced on each side of the reaction. Balancing means the total number of atoms stays the same, but their arrangement within specific reactants and products can change. The law of conservation of matter states that matter can never be created or destroyed. Heat may be absorbed or released in a reaction; these are classified as endothermic and exothermic reactions, respectively. The rate of the reaction increases with temperature for most reactions.

126. C: Igneous rock. Fossils are least likely to be found in igneous rock. Igneous rock is formed by extreme heat as magma escapes through the Earth's crust and cools. The remains of plants and animals in fossil form are not usually preserved under these conditions. Sedimentary rock is where the abundance of fossils are found. Sedimentary rock is formed more slowly and is very abundant. Since soft mud and silts compress into layers, organisms can also be deposited. Metamorphic rock is rock that has undergone change by heat and pressure. This usually destroys any fossils, but occasionally fossil remains are distorted and can be found in metamorphic rock.

127. B: It is true that rocks are classified by their formation and the minerals they contain, while minerals are classified by their chemical composition and physical properties. Choice A is incorrect because rocks may contain traces of organic compounds. Choices C and D are incorrect because only minerals can be polymorphs and only rocks contain mineraloids.

128. D: It has a different number of neutrons than its element. An isotope is a variation of an element that has a different number of neutrons. The element and its various isotopes continue to have the same numbers of protons and electrons. For example, carbon has three naturally occurring isotopes, carbon-12, carbon-13 and carbon-14, which is radioactive. Isotopes of an element differ in mass number, which is the number of protons and neutrons added together, but have the same atomic number, or number of protons.

129. B: Cool the liquid. If a gas and a liquid are placed in a sealed container, cooling the liquid will help dissolve the gas into the liquid. Gasses have higher solubility in liquids at lower temperatures. At higher temperatures, the gas molecules will have more kinetic energy and will have enough energy to overcome intermolecular interactions with the liquid solvent and leave the solution. This also explains why heating the liquid is incorrect. Shaking the container is also incorrect as this would give the gas energy to escape. Decreasing the pressure on the lid may or may not significantly affect the pressure inside the vessel depending on the nature of the vessel, but decreasing the pressure inside the vessel would decrease the solubility of the gas in the liquid.

130. B: Lower. The freezing point of seawater is lower than that of fresh water as sea water is denser. It is denser because it has more dissolved salts. The freezing point changes with salinity, pressure, and density, but can be as low as -2°C (28.4°F), compared with 0°C (32°F) for fresh water.

131. C: Tropical climate zones are characterized by frequent rainfall, especially during the monsoon season, and by moderate temperatures that vary little from season to season or between night and day. Tropical zones do experience frequent rainfall, which leads to abundant vegetation.

132. D: Decay. The process whereby a radioactive element releases energy slowly over a long period of time to lower its energy and become more stable is best described as decay. The nucleus undergoing decay, known as the parent nuclide, spontaneously releases energy most commonly through the emission of an alpha particle, a beta particle or a gamma ray. The changed nucleus, called the daughter nuclide, is now more stable than the parent nuclide, although the daughter nuclide may undergo another decay to an even more stable nucleus. A decay chain is a series of decays of a radioactive element into different more stable elements.

133. A: Lysosomes. A lysosome is an organelle that contains digestive enzymes that break down food and unneeded substances and are thought to be linked to the aging process. Chromatin is the structure created by DNA and various proteins in the cell nucleus during interphase and condenses to form chromosomes. Plastids are found in plants and algae. They often contain pigments and usually help make chemical compounds for the plant. The Golgi apparatus prepares macromolecules like proteins and lipids for transport.

134. C: The slope is very steep. On a topographic map, an area where the contour lines are very close together indicates that the slope is very steep. Lines very far apart would indicate a more gradual change in elevation. Contour lines help represent the actual shape of the Earth's surface features and geographic landmarks like rivers, lakes and vegetation. Topographic maps also show man-made features such as roads, dams, and major buildings. They are based on aerial photography and the quadrangle maps are produced in various scales. The 7.5-minute quadrangle is very common and provides a 1:24,000 scale, where 1 inch represents 2,000 feet.

135. A: The distance from the Earth to the Sun is equal to one astronomical unit. An astronomical unit (AU) is equal to 93 million miles and is far smaller than a light year or a parsec. A light year is defined as the distance light can travel in a vacuum in one year, and is equal to roughly 64,341 AU. A parsec is the parallax of one arcsecond and is equal to 206.26×10^3 astronomical units.

136. D: Sound cannot travel through a vacuum, though it doesn't necessarily follow that it *can* travel through solids. Nor does the fact sound can travel through a solid follow from the fact that the atoms are packed tightly together. The fact that a sound is produced by knocking on a solid object also does not prove sound can pass through the object. However, if you hear a sound on the other side of a solid wall, the sound must have traveled through the wall. Choice D is the best answer.

137. A: Anthophyta. Anthophyta is a division of plants that produces seeds as part of reproduction. Anthophyta are also known as the group that contains flowering plants. It is the largest and most diverse grouping of plants and includes many food, clothing and medicinal uses for humans. Grains, beans, nuts, fruits, vegetables, spices, tea, coffee, chocolate, cotton, linen, and aspirin are all derived from plants from anthophyta. Lycophyta is a small group of plants including club mosses and scale trees. Sphenophyta contains about 30 species including horsetails, foxtails, or scouring rushes. Pterophyta contains non-seed plants like ferns. Lycophyta, sphenophyta, and pterophyta all use spores to reproduce sexually.

138. A: A magnetic field is created by a spin magnetic dipole moment and the orbital magnetic dipole moment of the electrons in atoms. Therefore, it is the spinning and rotating of electrons in atoms that creates a magnetic field. Choice B describes the nucleus and electron clouds within an atom. Choice C creates thermal energy. Choice D creates a good electrical conductor.

139. D: The asteroid belt in our solar system is located between Mars and Jupiter. The asteroid belt is populated by asteroids and dwarf planets that are distributed thinly enough that spacecraft can pass through the belt with relative ease.

140. D: Voltage is the same for each path and current is greatest in path C. In a parallel circuit, the voltage is the same for all three paths. Because the resistance is different on each path but the voltage is the same, Ohm's law dictates that the current will also be different for each path. Ohm's

94

law says that current is inversely related to resistance. Therefore, the current will be greatest in path C as it has the least resistance, 2 ohms.

Practice Test #3

1. Ms. Baird wants to check her students' individual comprehension skills, specifically their ability to support an idea with evidence from a text. Which scenario is the best way to accomplish her goals?

    a. Split the students into groups after reading the text as a class and allow them to work together on a worksheet activity she has designed.
    b. Play a game in which Ms. Baird posts a card with a main idea. Students read silently and independently and raise their hands to answer when they have found a transition in the plot.
    c. As a class, brainstorm main ideas, topics, or concepts from a text. Allow students to choose a select number of these ideas and copy them onto separate index cards. The students then should individually review the text, recording any supporting evidence on the notecard with the applicable main idea.
    d. Administer a comprehension quiz during class. Allow students to switch papers and grade each other's work. Next, students can spend the remainder of the class period discussing the answers so that each one understands the text fully.

2. Another name for a persuasive essay is:

    a. Dynamic essay
    b. Convincing essay
    c. Argumentative essay
    d. Position paper

3. The teacher and her students brainstorm a list of talents, skills, and specialized knowledge belonging to members of the class. Some of the items on the list include how to make a soufflé, how to juggle, and how to teach a dog to do tricks. One student knows a great deal about spiders and another about motorcycles. She asks each student to write an essay about something he or she is good at or knows a great deal about. What kind of essay is she asking the students to produce?

    a. Cause and effect
    b. Compare/contrast
    c. Example
    d. Argumentative

4. What is the primary reason the early 21st century has been referred to as the Information Age?

    a. Because educational and governmental agencies require greater information
    b. Because there are more sources and outputs of information than ever before
    c. Because students can now learn all they need to know in four years of college
    d. Because college students today are much more interested in new information

5. Which choice constitutes the best method for building conceptual vocabulary?

    a. Using word webs to organize thinking about related terms
    b. Previewing vocabulary words for upcoming units in other subjects such as science or social studies
    c. Implementing a framework for introducing students to various concepts over time
    d. Practicing sight words

6. A third-grade teacher has several students reading above grade level. Most of the remaining students are reading at grade level. There are also a few students reading below grade level. She decides to experiment. Her hypothesis is that by giving the entire class a chapter book above grade level, high-level readers will be satisfied, grade-level readers will be challenged in a positive way, and students reading below grade level will be inspired to improve. Her method is most likely to:

    a. Succeed, producing students reading at an Instructional reading level. High-level readers will be happy to be given material appropriate to their reading level. Grade-level readers will challenge themselves to improve reading strategies in order to master the text. Because only a few of the students are reading below grade level, the other students, who feel happy and energized, will inspire the slower readers by modeling success.

    b. Succeed, producing students reading at an Independent reading level. High-level readers will independently help grade-level readers who will, in turn, independently help those below grade level.

    c. Fail, producing students at a Frustration reading level. Those reading below grade level are likely to give up entirely. Those reading at grade level are likely to get frustrated and form habits that will actually slow down their development.

    d. Fail, producing students reading at a Chaotic reading level. By nature, children are highly competitive. The teacher has not taken into consideration multiple learning styles. The children who are at grade level will either become bitter and angry at those whose reading level is above grade level or simply give up. The children reading below grade level will not be able to keep up and will in all likelihood act out their frustration or completely shut down.

7. A teacher is working with a group of English Language Learners. She asks them to take two pieces of paper. At the top of the first paper, they are to write *SAME*, at the top of the other, *DIFFERENT*. Each child will consider what his native country and the United States have in common, and what distinct features each country possesses. The children are using which method in organizing their ideas?

    a. Hunt and peck
    b. Consider and persuade
    c. Evaluate and contrast
    d. Compare and contrast

8. When making in-text citations in a research paper, which of the following reflects MLA guidelines for citing Web sources with regard to page numbers?

    a. If a Web source does not include pagination, you are advised to avoid citing that source.
    b. If page numbers appear on a printout from a website, include these numbers in citations.
    c. In-text citations of online sources in research papers should never include page numbers.
    d. If the Web source is a PDF file, it is recommended to cite page numbers in your citations.

9. English language learner (ELL) students typically are able to develop which type of English language skills the soonest?

    a. They typically develop BICS much sooner than CALP.
    b. They typically develop CALP more quickly than BICS.
    c. They typically develop both at about the same rates.
    d. They develop these at individually varying speeds.

10. Dr. Jenks is working with a group of students. They are about to read a science book about fossils. Before they begin, she writes the words *stromatolites, fossiliferous,* and *eocene* on the board. She explains the meaning of each word. These words are examples of:

    a. Academic words
    b. Alliteration
    c. Content-specific words
    d. Ionization

11. The phrase "Pretty as a picture" is *best* described as a:

    a. Metaphor
    b. Simile
    c. Duodenum's couple
    d. Figure of speech

12. Which of the following statements is most accurate about writing the introduction to an essay or paper?

    a. The introduction should use the technique of starting essays with dictionary definitions.
    b. The introduction should leave the most attention-getting material for later in the work.
    c. The introduction should move from the focused and specific to the broad and general.
    d. The introduction should move from the broad and general to the focused and specific.

13. A school has a policy of only permitting administration of its first choice among standardized formal assessments of phonological development twice per school year to conserve money and time. A 1st-grade teacher wanting to inform her instructional planning, implementation, and adjustments appropriately can do which of these?

    a. Stick to the school's policy and do the best she can with the results
    b. Lobby administrators to change policy to giving this test more often
    c. Use informal assessments continually and exclusively
    d. Conduct informal and other formal assessments on an ongoing basis

14. Phonemic awareness is a type of:

    a. Phonological awareness. Phonemic awareness is the ability to recognize sounds within words
    b. Phonics. It is a teaching technique whereby readers learn the relationship between letters and sounds
    c. Alphabetization. Unless a reader knows the alphabet, phonemic awareness is useless
    d. Syntactical awareness. Understanding the underlying structure of a sentence is key to understanding meaning

15. The purpose of "targeted instruction" is to:

    a. Deliver instructions that are precise, clear, and direct so that students understand exactly what is expected
    b. Accurately rank a group of learners from low achievers to high achievers so that the teacher knows from the beginning of the school year which students have less ability and will, therefore, need support
    c. Teach students how to take information from a text and reorganize it into bulleted lists
    d. Assess and target areas needing improvement as well as areas of greatest strength for each student to ensure that all members of a class are receiving instruction tailored to their specific needs

16. In writing, _____ is the overall written expression of the writer's attitude, and _____ is the individual way in which the writer expresses the former.

    a. Voice; tone
    b. Tone; voice
    c. Style; tone
    d. Voice; style

17. Which of the following literary elements are most likely to be found in *both* fictional narratives *and* nonfictional informational text?

    a. The writing style of the author
    b. Labeled diagrams and photos
    c. Excitement and drama
    d. Themes and plots

18. *Train, brain, spring.* The underlined letters are examples of:

    a. Consonant digraph
    b. Consonant blend
    c. Consonant shift
    d. Continental shift

19. A student is taking a reading test. The teacher has blocked out a number of words. Each blank is assigned a set of three possible words. The student must select the correct word from each set so that the text makes sense. The student is taking:

    a. A clover test
    b. A maze test
    c. A flower exam
    d. A PRE test

20. A writing assignment asks the student to do things like organize, plan, formulate, assemble, compose, construct, or arrange some material they have read or learned. Which of the following cognitive (learning) objectives is the teacher aiming to meet with this assignment?

    a. Analysis
    b. Synthesis
    c. Evaluation
    d. Application

21. Following a typical developmental sequence, which of the following is expected of 2nd-graders in decoding and identifying new or unfamiliar words?

    a. Identifying new words and compound words via phonics, roots, suffixes, and analogies
    b. Identifying new word meanings through knowledge of familiar synonyms and antonyms
    c. Identifying new word meanings by comparing to known homophones and homographs
    d. Identifying new word meanings by roots, prefixes, suffixes, idioms, and dictionary markings

22. "Decoding" is also called:

    a. Remediation
    b. Deciphering
    c. Alphabetic principle
    d. Deconstruction

23. A high school teacher has given her students an assignment to write a non-rhyming poem of three lines. The first and last lines each contain five syllables, and the middle line contains seven syllables. The students are writing a:

    a. Limerick
    b. Metaphor
    c. Villanelle
    d. Haiku

24. Which of the following would be most useful in assessing and documenting students' language progress throughout a school year?

    a. An audio/video recording of each student reading the same text at the beginning of the year and again at the end of the year
    b. A portfolio including pre-tests, post-tests, vocabulary work, journal entries, writing assignments, group projects and other relevant work from throughout the year
    c. Score composites and details from state- and national-referenced exams or other standardized tests.
    d. A detailed narrative composed by the student's teacher, detailing strengths, weaknesses, and descriptions of the student's work.

25. Of the following statements, which is true about the relationship of reading fluency, word decoding, and reading comprehension?

    a. Developing fluency in reading has no relationship to speed and automaticity with decoding words.
    b. Students should have strong word recognition foundations established before fluency instruction.
    c. Reading fluency shows faster information processing speed, but has no impact on comprehension.
    d. Slower, less automatic word decoding decreases reading fluency, but it increases comprehension.

26. A reading teacher is assessing a fifth grader to determine her reading level. Timed at a minute, the student reads with 93% accuracy. She misreads an average of seven words out of 100. What is her reading level?

    a. She is reading at a Frustration level
    b. She is reading at an Excellence level
    c. She is reading at an Instructional level
    d. She is reading at an Independent level

27. A distinguishing feature of the form known as haiku is

    a. 5/7/5 syllables per line
    b. An ABA rhyme scheme
    c. Perfectly regular meter
    d. Lengthy epic narratives

28. Which of the following statements is most true?

a. Introducing oral and written texts from a variety of cultures can enhance students' understanding and appreciation of language.
b. Children typically learn language best when exposed primarily to texts exemplary of their own background or culture, thereby increasing their ability to identify personally with what they are learning.
c. Studying other languages will impair a student's ability to develop his or her own first language.
d. Students should be exposed to one type of text at a time to diminish genre confusion.

29. A teacher writes four sentences on the board and instructs his students to copy the sentences from the board into their notebooks. They must capitalize words with suffixes. Which sentence is correct?

a. The PRINCE declared his undying love for the PRINCESS.
b. Television is a form of MULTIMEDIA.
c. This loud, loud noise is very DISPLEASING.
d. The BOOKKEEPER examined every page of the rare play.

30. Which of the following statements regarding the acquisition of language is false?

a. Young children often have the ability to comprehend written language just as early as they can comprehend or reproduce oral language when given appropriate instruction
b. Oral language typically develops before a child understands the relationship between spoken and written word
c. Most young children are first exposed to written language when an adult reads aloud
d. A child's ability to speak, read, and write depends on a variety of physiological factors, as well as environmental factors

31. Relative to reading, we should teach students to activate their prior knowledge at which time(s)?

a. Before reading
b. During reading
c. After reading
d. All of the above

32. A classroom is comprised of students with varying abilities in language. Some students can read fluently while others are still just learning. Speech and language abilities also range widely among the students. Which approach best suits this class?

a. Each student begins with reading texts slightly below their ability level and practices reading aloud with partners and teachers to build skills.
b. The teacher consistently presents challenging material for students, knowing that when students are held to high expectations, they typically rise to meet a challenge.
c. The teacher splits the classroom into groups based on ability and appoints a group leader to guide other students.
d. The class is exposed to a variety of "texts," in combination with direct phonetic and vocabulary instruction, including written text, video, song, and spoken stories.

33. To help students understand abstract concepts in the print materials they read, which instructional aids that teachers provide can students *always* use three-dimensionally?

    a. Examples
    b. Manipulatives
    c. Graphic organizers
    d. Charts, tables, graphs

34. Examples of CVC words include:

    a. Add, pad, mad
    b. Cat, tack, act
    c. Elephant, piano, examine
    d. Dog, sit, leg

35. In first-language (L1) and second-language (L2) acquisition, which of the following is true about developmental stages?

    a. L2 learners do not undergo the first stage called the Silent Period as L1 learners do.
    b. L2 learners undergo all stages but are urged to skip the first stage more than in L1s.
    c. L2 learners do not undergo the second stage of Formulaic Speech as L1 learners do.
    d. L2 learners undergo the third stage of Structural and Semantic Simplifications later.

36. Which of the following is the best use of technology in a language arts classroom?

    a. Providing laptops to students to achieve more effective note-taking, access to word processing programs, and access to the internet.
    b. Encouraging the use of PowerPoint or similar programs to support lectures and oral presentations, as well as to organize pertinent class concepts.
    c. Incorporating a computer-based "language lab" in which students can listen to texts and engage in interactive word-study and comprehension activities.
    d. Whenever possible, watching film interpretations based on texts studied in class.

37. Which of the following is the correct sequence of these phases of spelling development?

    a. Semiphonetic, precommunicative, transitional, correct, phonetic
    b. Precommunicative, semiphonetic, phonetic, transitional, correct
    c. Correct, phonetic, semiphonetic, precommunicative, transitional
    d. Phonetic, semiphonetic, transitional, correct, precommunicative

38. Context clues are useful in:

    a. Predicting future action
    b. Understanding the meaning of words that are not familiar
    c. Understanding character motivation
    d. Reflecting on a text's theme

39. Of the following, which statement is correct regarding Standard English?

    a. The formal Standard English applies to written language.
    b. Standard English is universal in English-speaking nations.
    c. Speech communities use the Standard English of writing.
    d. The Standard English construct does not include dialects.

40. Which choice is the best method of structuring language arts curriculum and instruction?

a. Examine all state-level or national standardized tests that students will be required to take. Structure the curriculum and lessons to address all concepts included in the tests, with an attempt to proportion the time spent in a way that mirrors the breakdown of the tests.

b. Research the instructional methods used in supplemental education fields. Use those newer methods of introducing and reinforcing concepts in class to ensure that students are receiving consistent and standard instruction.

c. Use the written curriculum provided by the school district or specific campus as a foundation for instruction. Schedule regular planning sessions to incorporate a variety of texts and instruction methods, as well as to coordinate instruction with teachers of other subjects.

d. Plan sequential units of study that focus on isolated skills such as word and vocabulary study, comprehension strategies, listening, viewing, and speaking. Design lessons to focus on the mastery of one skill at a time with the goal of studying the relationship between skills toward the end of the school year.

41. Expectations for middle school students, including 6th-graders, which of the following is *not* an included expectation?

a. To interpret and understand visual imagery, meanings, and messages
b. To conduct analyses and critiques of how visual media are important
c. To produce visual media representations communicating with others
d. To get ideas from the environment, and develop and organize them

42. Syllable types include:

a. Closed, open, silent e, vowel team, vowel-r, and consonant-le
b. Closed, open, silent, double-vowel, r, and le
c. Closed, midway, open, emphasized, prefixed, and suffixed
d. Stressed, unstressed, and silent

43. The English language word "noob" is an example of the result of which linguistic process?

a. Blending
b. Conversion
c. Neologisms
d. Onomatopoeia

44. A teacher designs lessons for the upcoming week. During the first part of the week, the teacher is going to divide the class into two sections. While one group is working independently on their projects, the other group will sit in a circle. The teacher has broken a story up into several sections that each student will read a section aloud. The teacher will note for her records how many errors a student makes. She will also administer a brief verbal "quiz" to which the students will respond in writing. The combination of verbal reading results and comprehension quiz results will give her a better understanding of each child's abilities and/or needs. What kind of assessment did this teacher use?

a. Cloze-style
b. Informal reading inventory
c. Student response form
d. Articulation assessment

45. Among assessments of reading comprehension, which of these compares student scores to the average scores of a sample of students representing the same population?

    a. A norm-referenced state test
    b. An informal reading inventory
    c. A curriculum-based assessment
    d. A criterion-referenced state test

46. Word-recognition ability is:

    a. Equally important to all readers
    b. Used only by fluent readers
    c. Another term for "word attack"
    d. Especially important to English Language Learners and students with reading disabilities

47. Which choice describes a primary benefit of an adult's reading aloud to a group of elementary students?

    a. Students have a chance to rest their minds and enjoy oral language.
    b. The adult can model reading fluently for students still building reading skills.
    c. Students have time and opportunity to work on individual projects and assignments while listening to the story.
    d. The adult transmits a great deal of conceptual knowledge via auditory instruction, which is especially beneficial for students who are auditory learners.

48. A dartboard consists of two concentric circles with radii of 3 inches and 6 inches. If a dart is thrown onto the board, what is the probability the dart will land in the inner circle?

    a. $\frac{1}{4}$
    b. $\frac{1}{2}$
    c. $\frac{1}{3}$
    d. $\frac{1}{5}$

49. A ball has a diameter of 7 inches. Which of the following best represents the volume?

    a. 165.7 in^3
    b. 179.6 in^3
    c. 184.5 in^3
    d. 192.3 in^3

50. Which of the following pairs of equations represents the lines of symmetry in the figure below?

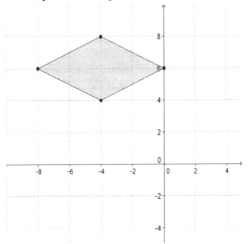

a. $x = -4, y = 6$
b. $x = 4, y = 6$
c. $y = -4, x = 6$
d. $y = 4, x = -6$

51. Which of these graphs is **NOT** representative of the data set shown below?

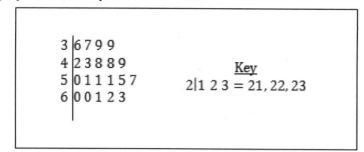

```
3 | 6 7 9 9
4 | 2 3 8 8 9
5 | 0 1 1 1 5 7
6 | 0 0 1 2 3
```

Key
2|1 2 3 = 21, 22, 23

a.

b.

c.

d. All of these graphs represent the data set.

52. Zeke drove from his house to a furniture store in Atlanta and then back home along the same route. It took Zeke three hours to drive to the store. By driving an average of 20 mph faster on his return trip, Zeke was able to save an hour of driving time. What was Zeke's average driving speed on his round trip?

a. 24 mph
b. 48 mph
c. 50 mph
d. 60 mph

53. For which of these does a rotation of 120° about the center of the polygon map the polygon onto itself?

    a. Square
    b. Regular hexagon
    c. Regular octagon
    d. Regular decagon

54. Marlon pays $45 for a jacket that has been marked down 25%. What was the original cost of the jacket?

    a. $80
    b. $75
    c. $65
    d. $60

55. Aidan has a plastic container in the shape of a square pyramid. He wants to fill the container with chocolate candies. If the base has a side length of 6 inches and the height of the container is 9 inches, how many cubic inches of space may be filled with candies?

    a. 98
    b. 102
    c. 108
    d. 112

56. Mr. Sarver, a second-grade teacher, notices that a few of his students are struggling with the concept of borrowing when subtracting two digit numbers. Which of the following activities would best help students understand this concept of borrowing?

    a. The teacher works subtraction problems on the white board.
    b. The students watch a children's video about borrowing.
    c. The students complete a worksheet with subtraction problems.
    d. The students use cardboard manipulatives to model subtraction problems.

57. Coach Weybright's 6th-grade basketball team has played 36 games this season. The ratio of wins to losses is 2:1. If x represents the number of wins, which of the following proportions can be used to determine the number of wins?

    a. $\dfrac{x}{36} = \dfrac{2}{1}$
    b. $\dfrac{x}{2} = \dfrac{1}{36}$
    c. $\dfrac{x}{3} = \dfrac{36}{2}$
    d. $\dfrac{x}{36} = \dfrac{2}{3}$

58. Mr. Orr asks his class to use inductive reasoning as to determine the pattern in this series of numbers. Which number is next in this series?

      2, 5, 10, 17, ___

    a. 25
    b. 26
    c. 22
    d. 24

59. Given that the two horizontal lines in the diagram below are parallel, which pair of angles is congruent?

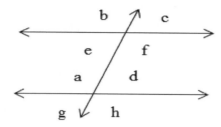

a. e and b
b. d and h
c. g and c
d. d and f

60. Which number comes next in the sequence?

16, 24, 34, 46, 60

a. 72
b. 74
c. 76
d. 56

61. The set $\{a, b, c, d\}$ forms a group under operation #. Which of these statements is (are) true about the group?

#	a	b	c	d
a	c	d	b	a
b	d	c	a	b
c	b	a	d	c
d	a	b	c	d

I. The identity element of the group is d.
II. The inverse of c is c.
III. The operation # is commutative.

a. I
b. III
c. I, III
d. I, II, III

62. In how many distinguishable ways can a family of five be seated at a circular table with five chairs if Tasha and Mac must be kept separated?

a. 6
b. 12
c. 24
d. 60

63. Which of the following steps were applied to ΔABC?

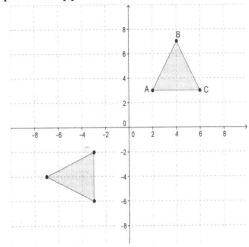

    a. reflection across the x-axis and rotation of 90 degrees
    b. reflection across the x-axis and rotation of 180 degrees
    c. reflection across the x-axis and rotation of 270 degrees
    d. reflection across the y-axis and rotation of 180 degrees

64. Miss Wise asks her students to work in pairs to construct Venn diagrams which classify rational numbers, irrational numbers, real numbers, and integers. As she walks around the room to observe their progress, which of the following criterion could she use to assess the students' understanding of these sets of numbers?

    a. The set of integers should include the other three sets.
    b. The set of rational numbers should include the other three sets.
    c. The set of irrational numbers should include the other three sets.
    d. The set of real numbers should include the other three sets.

65. During a unit on geometry, Ms. Nifong instructs her student to sketch two congruent polygons. Which of the following sketches completes this task correctly?

    a. Two rectangles with the same perimeter
    b. Two polygons with the same shape
    c. Two polygons with the same side lengths
    d. Two squares with the same area

66. What is the area of the figure graphed below?

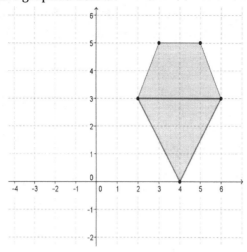

    a. 11 units²
    b. 11.5 units²
    c. 12 units²
    d. 12.5 units²

67. Which system of linear inequalities has no solution?
    a. $x - y < 3$ and $x - y \geq -3$
    b. $y \leq 6 - 2x$ and $\frac{1}{3}y + \frac{2}{3}x \geq 2$
    c. $6x + 2y \leq 12$ and $3x \geq 8 - y$
    d. $x + 4y \leq -8$ and $y + 4x > -8$

68. What is the constant of proportionality represented by the table below?

x	y
2	−8
5	−20
7	−28
10	−40
11	−44

    a. −12
    b. −8
    c. −6
    d. −4

69. Ms. Alejo is teaching a unit on fractions to her third-grade class. Some students are completing an activity in identifying the parts of a fraction. Others are completing an activity on equivalent fractions. Another group of students is completing an activity on adding and subtracting fractions. Which of the following instruction methods describes the various readiness levels Ms. Alejo is incorporating?
    a. Collaborative learning
    b. Small group instruction
    c. Nonlinguistic representations
    d. Differentiated instruction

70. During an activity, Mrs. Schwartz instructs her students to place groups of coins in order of decreasing value. Which of the following students correctly completed this activity?

  a. Henry with Group 1: 2 dimes, 2 nickels, and 4 pennies; Group 2: 1 dime, 3 nickels, 2 pennies; Group 3: 1 dime, 2 nickels, 7 pennies
  b. Graham with Group 1: 1 dime, 5 nickels, and 5 pennies; Group 2: 2 dimes, 2 nickels, 8 pennies; Group 3: 1 dime, 2 nickel, 9 pennies
  c. Landon with Group 1: 3 dimes, 4 nickels, and 9 pennies; Group 2: 2 dimes, 4 nickels, 3 pennies; Group 3: 1 dime, 9 nickels, 4 pennies
  d. Elizabeth with Group 1: 2 dimes, 3 nickels, and 6 pennies; Group 2: 2 dimes, 4 nickels, 1 penny; Group 3: 1 dime, 1 nickel, 7 pennies

71. What is the length of the hypotenuse in the triangle shown below?

  a. 4 cm
  b. $8\sqrt{3}$ cm
  c. 16 cm
  d. $8\sqrt{2}$ cm

72. A cube inscribed in a sphere has a volume of 64 cubic units. What is the volume of the sphere in cubic units?

  a. $4\pi\sqrt{3}$
  b. $8\pi\sqrt{3}$
  c. $32\pi\sqrt{3}$
  d. $256\pi\sqrt{3}$

73. Mandy can buy 4 containers of yogurt and 3 boxes of crackers for $9.55. She can buy 2 containers of yogurt and 2 boxes of crackers for $5.90. How much does one box of crackers cost?

  a. $1.75
  b. $2.00
  c. $2.25
  d. $2.50

74. Which of the following describes how to find the formula for the volume of a regular solid prism?

  a. Find the perimeter of the base of the prism and multiply by the height of the prism.
  b. Find the area of the base of the prism and multiply by the height of the prism.
  c. Find the sum of the areas of the faces and multiply by the length of the prism.
  d. Find the sum of the areas of the lateral faces and multiply by the number of faces.

75. $A = \{3, -4, 1\}$ and $B = \{0, 5, 9, 2\}$. What is $A \cap B$?

    a. $\{3, -4, 1, 0, 5, 9, 2\}$
    b. $\{-4, 2, 3\}$
    c. $\{0, 1, 2, 3, 5, 9\}$
    d. $\varnothing$

76. Which of these would best illustrate change over time?

    a. Pie chart
    b. Line graph
    c. Box-and-whisker plot
    d. Venn diagram

77. Which of the following activities would best help first-grade students understand the concept of measuring objects?

    a. Measuring the height of the pencil sharpener using a meter stick
    b. Measuring the length of the chalkboard using a tape measure
    c. Measuring the width of their desks using dominoes placed end to end
    d. Measuring the circumference of the trash can be using a cloth tape

78. The two prisms shown below are similar. What is the measurement of x?

    a. $4\frac{3}{4}$ in
    b. $5\frac{1}{3}$ in
    c. $5\frac{2}{3}$ in
    d. $5\frac{3}{4}$ in

79. Kim's current monthly rent is $800. She is moving to another apartment complex, where the monthly rent will be $1,100. What is the percent increase in her monthly rent amount?

    a. 25.5%
    b. 27%
    c. 35%
    d. 37.5%

80. A sixth-grade teacher asks her students to find the error in this algebra problem. What is the error?

$$3x + 4x = (2^2 + 1) + 2(2)$$
$$7x = 5 + 2(2)$$
$$7x = 7(2)$$
$$7x = 14$$
$$x = 2$$

    a. The student incorrectly added before multiplying.
    b. The student incorrectly multiplied before adding.
    c. The student incorrectly applied the exponent.
    d. The student incorrectly combined like terms.

81. Which of the following is the graph of the equation $y = -4x - 6$?

a.

b.

c.

d.

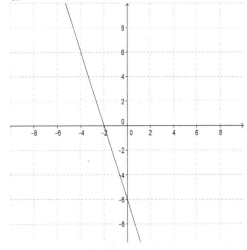

82. Andrea must administer $\frac{1}{12}$ of a medicine bottle to a patient. If the bottle contains $3\frac{4}{10}$ fluid ounces of medicine, how much medicine should be administered?

    a. $\frac{17}{60}$ fluid ounces

    b. $\frac{15}{62}$ fluid ounces

    c. $\frac{3}{19}$ fluid ounces

    d. $\frac{17}{67}$ fluid ounces

83. Which of the following options represents equivalency between mathematical expressions?

    a. $3 + x + 3x + 3 + x = 5x + 6$
    b. $7x - 2x = 9x$
    c. $2y + 2y + 2y = 6y^3$
    d. $2.5(x + 2) = 2.5x + 2$

84. Kendra uses the pie chart below to represent the allocation of her annual income. Her annual income is $40,000.

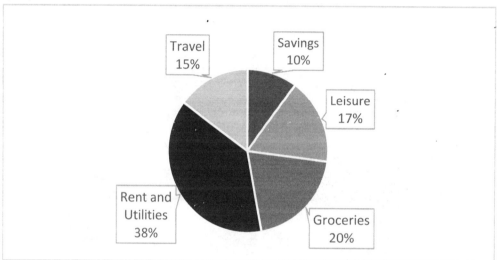

Which of the following statements is true?

    a. The amount of money she spends on travel and savings is more than $11,000.
    b. The amount of money she spends on rent and utilities is approximately $15,000.
    c. The amount of money she spends on groceries and savings is more than $13,000.
    d. The amount of money she spends on leisure is less than $5,000.

85. A newly introduced bill is first given to a _____ where it is either accepted, amended or rejected completely.

    a. Full committee
    b. Conference committee
    c. Subcommittee
    d. Senate committee

86. Which of the following is *not* true regarding the Virginia Companies?

    a. One of these companies, the Virginia Company of Plymouth, made its base in North America.
    b. One of these companies, the Virginia Company of London, made its base in Massachusetts.
    c. One company had a charter to colonize America between the Hudson and Cape Fear rivers.
    d. One company had a charter to colonize America from the Potomac River to north Maine.

87. Why was U.S. industrialization confined to the Northeast until after the Civil War?

    a. Because the Civil War delayed the development of water-powered manufacturing
    b. Because the Northeast had faster-running rivers than the rivers found in the South
    c. Because Slater's first cotton mill with horse-drawn production lost so much money
    d. Because the technical innovations for milling textiles had not as yet been invented

88. Unlike slaves, who were considered to be the property of their masters, most indentured servants in colonial times:

    a. Received wages for their labor.
    b. Were generally treated kindly by their employers.
    c. Were highly educated.
    d. Voluntarily entered into servitude.

89. Which of these was the greatest obstacle to success for the farmers who settled on the Great Plains in the latter part of the nineteenth century?

    a. The invention of barbed wire
    b. Passage of the Homestead Act
    c. Environmental conditions
    d. The Grange movement

90. Before the Civil War, to which of the following did Southern states object?

    a. An increase in Southern tobacco production
    b. An increase in tariffs on Northern manufactured goods
    c. An increase in western mining for gold
    d. An increase in the voting rights of slaves

91. Which of the following is *not* true about Democracy and the formation of the United States?

    a. The founding fathers stated in the Constitution that the USA would be a democracy
    b. The Declaration of Independence did not dictate democracy but stated its principles
    c. The United States Constitution stipulated that government be elected by the people
    d. The United States Constitution had terms to protect some, but not all, of the people

92. According to Karl Marx, two groups that are in continual conflict are:

    a. Farmers and landowners.
    b. Workers and owners.
    c. Kings and nobles.
    d. Politicians and voters.

93. The executive, legislative, and judicial branches of government compose:

    a. The federal government
    b. The democratic process
    c. Bicameralism
    d. Rule of law

94. Which of the following is *not* correct about the growth of America in the first half of the 19th century?

    a. By 1840, two-thirds of all Americans resided west of the Allegheny Mountains.
    b. The population of America doubled every 25 years during this time period.
    c. The trend of westward expansion increased as more people migrated west.
    d. Immigration to America from other countries was not substantial prior to 1820.

95. One reason the Articles of Confederation created a weak government was because it limited Congress's ability to do what?

    a. Declare war
    b. Conduct a census
    c. Vote
    d. Tax

96. Which of the following ancient civilizations of the Americas lived in Central America?

    a. The Incas
    b. The Aztecs
    c. All of these
    d. The Mayans

97. How was the Vice President chosen before the 12th Amendment was ratified?

    a. The President chose the Vice President
    b. Congress chose the Vice President
    c. The Vice President came in second in the Electoral College
    d. There was no Vice President

98. Which list of events is in the correct chronological order?

a.	c.
• French and Indian War • American Revolution • French Revolution • War of 1812	• French and Indian War • French Revolution • War of 1812 • American Revolution
b.	d.
• American Revolution • French Revolution • War of 1812 • French and Indian War	• French and Indian War • French Revolution • American Revolution • War of 1812

99. The Senate and the House of Representatives are an example of:

    a. Bicameralism
    b. Checks and balances
    c. Legislative oversight
    d. Federalism

100. If you know the longitude of a city in the United States, you can determine:

    a. The state in which it is located.
    b. The time zone in which it is located.
    c. Exactly how far it is from the equator.
    d. Approximate average winter temperature.

101. Which of the following best defines American GDP?

   a. The value, in American dollars, of all goods and services produced within American borders during one calendar year
   b. The value, in American dollars, of all goods and services produced by American companies during one calendar year
   c. The total value, in American dollars, of all American household incomes during one calendar year
   d. The value, in American dollars, of a "market basket" of goods and services in one year divided by the value of the same market basket in a previous year multiplied by 100

102. Representative democracy was likely motivated by:

   a. An increase in population
   b. Aristocracy
   c. The Supreme Court
   d. States passing laws that violated federal laws

103. Leading up to World War I, which group joined with the Triple Alliance after it formed?

   a. Austria–Hungary
   b. Germany
   c. Ottoman Empire
   d. Italy

104. The main purpose of the census is to:

   a. Monitor illegal immigration.
   b. Apportion seats in the House of Representatives.
   c. Help determine federal income tax rates.
   d. Reapportion seats in the United States Senate.

105. The impact of a transaction on parties not directly involved in the transaction is known as what?

   a. Social cost
   b. Social benefit
   c. Externality
   d. Marginal social cost

106. Which statement is *not* true regarding ancient Greek democracy?

   a. Democracy began to develop approximately 500 B.C.E.
   b. One of the first, best-known democracies was in Athens
   c. It was a direct democracy, not using any representatives
   d. It was a democracy completely open to all of the public

107. Which of the following is considered more a cause than an effect of the Industrial Revolution?

   a. Emergence of socialism
   b. Emergence of capitalism
   c. The Romantic movement
   d. The Protestant work ethic

117

108. The Underground Railroad was primarily:
    a. A route for abolitionists to smuggle weapons
    b. A route for slave owners to traffic slaves
    c. A means for slaves to travel to free states
    d. A strategy for state control of railway construction

109. What kind of chart would be best for representing the major events of World War I?
    a. Timeline
    b. Bar graph
    c. Pie chart
    d. Political map

110. Which of the following choices is/are *not* considered among causes of the French Revolution?
    a. Famines causing malnutrition and starvation
    b. War debt, Court spending, bad monetary system
    c. Resentment against the Catholic Church's rule
    d. Resentment against the Protestant Reformation

111. Which of the following is not true about Louis Pasteur?
    a. He made the first rabies vaccine
    b. He discovered the medical use for penicillin
    c. His experiments refuted the germ theory of disease
    d. He developed a process for reducing pathogens in food

112. How is a tie broken in the Senate?
    a. The Majority Whip casts the deciding vote
    b. The Speaker of the House votes
    c. They vote again
    d. The Vice President votes

113. Which of the following locations would be considered a modern cultural hearth?
    a. New York City, USA
    b. Baghdad, Iraq
    c. Auckland, New Zealand
    d. Edmonton, Canada

114. Which of the following materials has randomly aligned dipoles?
    a. a non-magnetic substance
    b. an electromagnet
    c. a permanent magnet
    d. a superconductor

115. Once a hypothesis has been verified and accepted, it becomes a _____.
    a. fact
    b. law
    c. conclusion
    d. theory

116. How does the tilt of Earth's axis cause seasons?

a. A hemisphere experiences fall and winter when that half of Earth is tilted away from the Sun. It experiences spring and summer when that half of Earth is tilted towards the Sun

b. A hemisphere experiences winter and spring when that half of Earth is tilted away from the Sun. It experiences summer and fall when that half of Earth is tilted towards the Sun ·

c. A hemisphere experiences spring and summer when that half of Earth is tilted away from the Sun. It experiences fall and winter when that half of Earth is tilted towards the Sun

d. A hemisphere experiences summer and fall when that half of Earth is tilted away from the Sun. It experiences winter and spring when that half of Earth is tilted towards the Sun

117. If a population reaches a maximum size and ceases to grow due to a limited availability of resources, the population is

a. unstable.
b. shrinking exponentially.
c. at carrying capacity.
d. moving towards extinction.

118. The center of an atom is called the ____. It is composed of ____.

a. nucleus; protons and neutrons.
b. nucleus; protons and electrons.
c. electron cloud; electrons and protons.
d. electron cloud; electrons and neutrons.

119. The volume of water in a bucket is 2.5 liters. When an object with an irregular shape and a mass of 40 grams is fully submerged in the water, the total volume becomes 4.5 liters. What is the density of the object?

a. 0.1 g/L
b. 2 g/L
c. 20 g/L
d. 80 g/L

120. Most organic molecules have all of the following properties except

a. high solubility in water.
b. a tendency to melt.
c. covalently bonded.
d. high flammability.

121. The formation of sedimentary rock includes all of the following processes except

a. layering.
b. cementation.
c. compaction.
d. heat.

122. Which of the following is usually the first form of study in a new area of scientific inquiry?

a. descriptive studies
b. controlled experiments
c. comparative data analysis
d. choosing a method and design

123. The specific heat capacity of ice is half as much as that of liquid water. What is the result of this?

a. It takes half the amount of energy to increase the temperature of a 1 kg sample of ice by 1°C than a 1 kg sample of water.
b. It takes twice the amount of energy to increase the temperature of a 1 kg sample of ice by 1°C than a 1 kg sample of water.
c. It takes a quarter the amount of energy to increase the temperature of a 1 kg sample of ice by 1°C than a 1 kg sample of water.
d. It takes the same amount of energy to increase the temperature of a 1 kg sample of ice and a 1 kg sample of water by 1°C.

124. Which statement best describes the molecular arrangement of a liquid crystal?

a. The molecular arrangement is random in some directions and regular in others.
b. The molecular arrangement is a regularly, repeating pattern in all directions.
c. The molecular arrangement is random in all directions.
d. The molecular arrangement is reduced to one layer with a random pattern.

125. Which statement best describes the process of absolute dating?

a. It compares the amount of radioactive material in a rock to the amount that has decayed into another element.
b. It measures the age of a rock by comparing it to fossils found in the same stratigraphic layer as the rock.
c. It measures the amount of daughter elements that have broken down by half.
d. It measures the mass loss of a rock by estimating the amount of material that has eroded due to catastrophic events.

126. The scientific method is a series of steps to ____.

a. solve a problem.
b. gather information.
c. ask a scientific question.
d. formulate a hypothesis.

127. Enzymes play an important role in the processes that help organisms stay healthy and survive. Which of the following BEST describes enzymes?

a. Enzymes are protein molecules that act as biological catalysts.
b. Enzymes are fat-soluble organic compounds with specific physiological functions.
c. Enzymes are strong acids that break down large biomolecules.
d. Enzymes are lipids that store energy.

128. Which statement accurately describes an electrolysis reaction?

a. A reaction that changes the charge of the atoms.
b. A reaction that uses electricity to drive it.
c. A reaction that creates electricity as a by-product.
d. A reaction that lowers the pH of the substances.

129. Which of the following does not control the movement of ocean currents?

a. Wind
b. Landmasses
c. Earth's rotation
d. Phase of the Moon

130. The majority of the solar energy that reaches Earth is absorbed by:

a. Glaciers.
b. Landmasses.
c. Oceans.
d. The Earth's atmosphere.

131. Electrons with greater amounts of energy are found _____ the nucleus than electrons with less energy.

a. closer to
b. farther from
c. more often inside
d. more randomly around

132. The main function of _____ is it to reduce the number of chromosomes to half the number of parent cells?

a. mitosis
b. telophase
c. meiosis I
d. meiosis II

133. If land cools off rapidly at night and the ocean water stays relatively warm, what type of wind is created?

a. Sea breeze
b. Land breeze
c. Monsoon
d. Trade wind

134. The structure of the Milky Way galaxy is best described as:

a. Spiral.
b. Starburst.
c. Elliptical.
d. Irregular.

135. A ball is resting on the front end of a boat. The boat is moving straight forward toward a dock. According to Newton's first law of motion, when the front of the boat hits the dock, how will the ball's motion change with respect to the boat?

a. The ball will remain at rest.
b. The ball will move backward.
c. The ball will move forward.
d. The ball will move upward.

136. In which taxonomic group are organisms most alike?

    a. Phylum
    b. Family
    c. Class
    d. Order

137. Which statement best explains the importance of recycling and using alternative sources of energy?

    a. It will lead to greater production of goods and consumer spending in the future.
    b. It will ensure the health and safety of populations and the long-term sustainability of the environment.
    c. It will get rid of human disease and end economic warfare in the future.
    d. It will allow fossil fuel supplies to be replenished for their continued use in the future.

138. Which of the following planets in our solar system is NOT a gas giant?

    a. Saturn
    b. Neptune
    c. Venus
    d. Jupiter

139. A scientist mixes two chemicals together, and they produce a violent reaction, generating considerable heat. Where did the thermal energy come from to heat up the chemicals?

    a. The kinetic energy of the molecules in the chemicals
    b. Potential energy inherent in the atomic bonds in the molecules of the chemicals
    c. It was absorbed from the surrounding air
    d. Nowhere; the energy was completely created by the reaction

140. Plants begin to break down the products of photosynthesis through respiration. What is the result of respiration?

    a. Water
    b. Oxygen and glucose
    c. Carbon dioxide and sugar
    d. Carbon dioxide and water

Answer Key and Explanations

1. C: The question prompt states that Ms. Baird wants to make sure her students understand certain concepts on an individual basis, rather than as a group. Choice C describes a scenario in which the students support each other in creating a foundation for the activity. They help each other and are scaffolded by their teacher in determining the main ideas. However, Ms. Baird utilizes the practice of silent reading to ensure that students are practicing the skill of finding supporting evidence on an individual level. She will be able to gauge each student's comprehension levels by checking their notecards after the lesson.

2. C: Argumentative essay. The goal of a persuasive essay is to convince the reader that the author's position or opinion on a controversial topic is correct. That opinion or position is called the argument. A persuasive essay argues a series of points, supported by facts and evidence.

3. C: Example. Example essays, also called illustration essays, are simple, straightforward pieces that depend on clearly described examples to make their points. An example essay isn't trying to convince the reader (argumentative), compare similar or dissimilar things (compare/contrast), or point to relationships such as cause and effect. Often, example essays teach the reader how to accomplish something or about something.

4. B: The early 21st century has been dubbed the Information Age primarily because, with widespread Internet use and other innovations in electronic communications and publishing, there are more sources of information and greater output of available information than ever before. While some agencies might require more information (A), this is only possible because such information is more readily available now. Professionals in higher education and research find that with this new explosion of information, college students cannot possibly gain enough information literacy by just reading texts and writing research papers, and cannot learn all they need to know in four years (C). This period is also not called the Information Age due to an increased student interest in acquiring information (D), but due to the increased access to information.

5. A: "Conceptual vocabulary" terms are related in meaning and often have complex meanings. For instance, the term "community" may refer simply to a group of people living in close proximity to one another. However, there are many ideas that can be associated with this concept: neighbors, helping, spending time with one another, roles within a community, and so on. Word webs can be used to show a central term and its related concepts, demonstrating the relationship between words based on meaning. Using this type of graphic organizer provides a tangible way to show students that some words have complex meanings and are interconnected with other aspects of language.

6. C: Fail, producing students at a Frustration reading level. Those reading below grade level are likely to give up entirely. Those reading at grade level are likely to get frustrated and form habits that will actually slow down their development. Giving students texts that are too far beyond their reach produces frustrated readers. In an effort to succeed, frustrated writers are likely to apply strategies that have worked for them in the past but cannot work in this case because the text is simply beyond them. Looking for contextual clues to understand the meaning of unfamiliar words requires that most of the words in the passage are familiar. Breaking unfamiliar words into individual phonemes or syllables can be effective, but not if the number of such words is excessive. In this case, students below reading level and students at reading level will become frustrated when the skills that have worked for them in the past now fail.

123

7. D: Compare and contrast. Asking children to write a list provides them with a visual model that is a side-by-side comparison of the two countries. In creating that visual model, each student first has to organize his or her thoughts mentally, deciding whether each particular item under consideration shares more or less in common with the other.

8. D: When online sources you are citing in your research paper are in PDFs and other file formats that have stable pagination, the MLA advises including the page number in the research paper's in-text citation because these numbers are valid and do not change. If a Web source has no pagination, as often happens, the MLA does NOT advise avoiding the citation (A); it advises simply making the citation without a page number because there is not one available. Unlike in PDFs (above), when citing a source from a printout, the MLA advises NOT including page numbers even if you see them because the same page numbers are not always found in all printouts (B). It is not true that in-text citations should never include page numbers (C).

9. A: Basic interpersonal communication skills (BICS) are language skills required in everyday social communication. These are less cognitively demanding, do not involve specialized vocabulary, typically take place in meaningful social contexts, and are necessary for social interaction. Cognitive academic language proficiency (CALP) is formal academic subject content language learning. CALP is more cognitively demanding, involves specialized subject vocabularies, takes place in academic contexts, and is necessary for school success. ELL students typically take 6 months to 2 years to develop adequate BICS, but at least 5-7 years to develop adequate CALP. If they had no formal education in their native languages and/or no second-language acquisition support, development may take 7-10 years.

10. C: Content-specific words. Because these words are specific to paleontology, it's unlikely the students know their meanings. Without understanding what these words mean, the students would not be able to understand the content of the passage they were about to read.

11. B: Simile. "Pretty as a picture" is a simile (comparison of two unlike things using the words *like* or *as*).

12. D: It is best to begin an essay or paper with a broader, more general introduction to the topic, and move to a more focused and specific point regarding the topic—not vice versa (C)—by the end of the introduction. This point is your thesis statement. Writing experts advise *against* the technique of beginning an essay with a dictionary definition (A) because it has been so overused that it has become ineffective and uninteresting. To engage the reader's interest in your topic, it is best to *begin* with some very attention-getting material rather than leaving it for later (B).

13. D: The most practical, thorough, and effective solution is to conduct informal assessments, as well as formal assessments other than the one the school has selected for biannual administration, to obtain continuing data on student phonological development to inform instructional planning, implementation, and adjustments according to student responses. Limiting assessment to the biennial formal test (A) will not provide enough information for individualizing instruction to each student's needs timely enough. Lobbying administrators to change policy (B) could work with some teachers and some administrators, but in many other cases would waste energy and time—and could strain teacher-administrator relations—without succeeding. Using informal assessments continually (C) is a good but not complete solution, whereas using both informal and other formal assessments continually (D) is.

14. A: Phonological awareness. Phonemic awareness is the ability to recognize sounds within words. Segmenting words and blending sounds are components of phonemic awareness.

Phonological awareness includes an understanding of multiple components of spoken language. Ability to hear individual words within a vocalized stream and ability to identify spoken syllables are types of phonological awareness.

15. D: Assess and target areas needing improvement as well as areas of greatest strength for each student to ensure that all members of a class are receiving instruction tailored to their specific needs.

16. B: Tone is the way in which the writer writes overall to express his or her attitude. Voice is who the reader hears speaking in the writing, the individual way the writer uses to express his or her tone—not vice versa (A). Style (options C and D) is the effect a writer creates through language, mechanics, and attitude or the sound (formal or informal) or impressions (seriousness, levity, grace, fluency) of the writing.

17. A: In both the fictional narrative genre and the nonfictional informational genre, the author will demonstrate some individual writing style; even very factual and objective expositional writing will reveal some personal stylistic characteristics. Labeled diagrams and photos (B) are more likely to be found in informational nonfiction. The majority of books with excitement and drama (C) are fictional narratives (some informational nonfiction books are presented in narrative form and include excitement, especially in children's literature, but these are the minority). Themes and plots (D) are also literary elements associated with fictional narrative.

18. B: Consonant blend. Consonant blend refers to a group of consonants in which each letter represents a separate sound.

19. B: A maze test. A maze test is a specific type of cloze test. In a cloze test, words are deleted and the reader must supply the missing words using contextual clues and vocabulary that is familiar. A maze test is a multiple-choice application of a cloze test.

20. B: The verbs listed here all refer to taking pieces or parts of information or knowledge and bringing them together to create a whole, and to building relationships among the parts to fit new or different circumstances. Analysis (A) is the opposite of synthesis—breaking information down into its component parts and demonstrating the relationships among those parts. An assignment for analysis would ask the student to compare, distinguish, test, categorize, examine, contrast, or analyze information. Evaluation (C) is making judgments of information based on given criteria, confirming or supporting certain preferences, and persuading the reader. An assignment targeting evaluation would use words like evaluate, predict, appraise, conclude, score, judge, or compare. Application (D) is using knowledge in new contexts. The assignment would ask the student to apply, prepare, practice, use, operate, sketch, calculate, solve, or illustrate.

21. B: According to many academic standards, 2nd-graders should be able to determine the meanings of new or unfamiliar words by comparing them to synonyms (words with similar meanings) and antonyms (words with opposite meanings). First-graders are expected to use phonics (letter-sound correspondences), word roots, word suffixes, and analogies (A) to decode words for reading. It is expected of 3rd-graders to use not only known synonyms and antonyms but additionally homophones (words sounding the same with different meanings) and homographs (words spelled the same but with different meanings) they know to discern new or unfamiliar word meanings (C). Determining word meanings by referring to word roots, prefixes, suffixes, idiomatic expressions, and familiar diacritical marks used in dictionaries (D) is expected of 4th-graders.

22. C: Alphabetic principle. The act of decoding involves first recognizing the sounds individual letters and letter groups make, and then blending the sounds to read the word. A child decoding the

125

word *spin*, for example, would first pronounce *sp/i/n* as individual sound units. She then would repeat the sounds, smoothly blending them. Because decoding involves understanding letters and their sounds, it is sometimes known as the alphabetic principle.

23. D: Haiku. Based on a Japanese form of poetry, haiku have become popular with students and teachers alike. Reading and writing haiku helps younger students become aware of syllables and helps older students learn about subtleties of vocabulary.

24. B: Assessment is an ongoing process that involves formal testing and a host of other methods. Students are working at any given time in the school year on a multitude of skills sets, and all of these skills are interrelated and developing simultaneously at different rates. It is impossible to ever provide a "snapshot" of a student's abilities because each student develops in a unique and complex manner. Choice A would only offer insight into a student's reading fluency. Choice C would show how a student could perform on standardized tests; however, many factors such as anxiety and test-taking speed affect those scores. Choice D relies on the teacher to interpret the student's strengths and weaknesses and would require an almost impossible attention to detail. Choice B includes both formal and informal assessments as well as giving insight into writing, vocabulary and other skill sets in a comprehensive portfolio.

25. B: Before beginning fluency instruction, typically not before halfway through the 1st grade at the earliest, teachers should ensure that students have strong word recognition skills to provide the necessary foundation. Student speed and automaticity in decoding individual words are directly related to developing reading fluency (A): rapid, automatic word decoding is the precursor to fluent reading. Reading fluency not only indicates faster information processing, it also has a direct impact on comprehension (C) because the faster a student can process information, the better the student can comprehend what s/he reads. When a student must decode words more slowly and less automatically, both reading fluency and comprehension are decreased (D): slow, conscious decoding does not increase comprehension by being more careful or thoughtful; instead, laborious student efforts to decode separate words for meaning divert the attention they could devote to overall comprehension if they could decode rapidly, effortlessly, and automatically.

26. C: She is reading at an Instructional level. In one minute, a student who misreads one or less than one word per twenty words, or with 95%–100% accuracy, is at an Independent reading level. A student who misreads one or less than one word per ten words, or with 90%–95% accuracy, is at an Instructional level. A student misreading more than one word out of ten, or with less than 90% accuracy, is at a Frustration level.

27. A: The haiku, originating in Japanese poetry and since adopted in English-language poetry, is a short poem of only three lines, often with 17 syllables, with the first and third lines having five syllables and the second line having seven syllables. (In Japanese there are many other rules, which become very complicated.) Haiku are typically unrhymed, so they do not have a rhyme scheme (B). Similarly, they do not employ any regular meter (C). Because haiku are typically 17 syllables or fewer, they do not involve long narratives (D).

28. A: Students are completely capable of understanding and appreciating oral traditions and written texts from other world cultures, as well as those originating from cultures in the students' own community. In fact, introducing a variety of material can increase some students' appreciation of language and literature as it enables them to learn about the world around them. Language skills emerge at a point in most children's development during which students are fascinated with learning new concepts. Introducing a variety of texts also benefits students in a classroom who belong to other cultures; these students are able to learn concepts from texts that represent their family, culture, or country of origin.

29. C: In Choice "a", the words prince and princess are capitalized, though they do not have suffixes. In choice "b", the word "multimedia" contains the prefix "multi", but no suffix. Choice "c" contains a word with the root "please," which also has both a prefix and a suffix. The "-ing" acts as the suffix in displeasing, therefore it is correctly capitalized.

30. A: Most adults can understand the relationship between oral and written language: components of oral language have representational symbols that can be written and decoded. However, most normally developing children acquire spoken language first and begin to develop reading and writing skills as they approach school-age. Many children are first exposed to the concept of written language when an adult introduces books or other written texts. However, a child's ability to read and write develops over time and is dependent on the development of physiological processes such as hearing, sight, and fine motor skills for writing. Written language development also typically requires direct instruction. Most children must be taught to read and write and rarely learn these skills simply by observing others.

31. D: Reading instructors should teach students to activate their prior knowledge because it will improve their reading comprehension. Before reading (choice A), teachers should discuss and model connections with existing knowledge to prepare students by helping them consider what they already know about the subject of the text. While they read (option B), students can make better sense of the text by considering how it fits with what they already know. After reading (choice C), teachers can lead discussions helping students focus on how the connections they made between the text and their previous knowledge informed their understanding of the text, and on how the text helped them build their foundations of existing knowledge.

32. D: Classrooms will most always consist of students at different levels of ability. The physical and psychological processes needed for reading evolve simultaneously over time and do so at different rates for each individual. No two students will match up perfectly with respect to language skills. Language skills also incorporate a variety of other processes, including speaking, listening, thinking, viewing, writing, and reading. By pairing direct instruction with various types of cognitive processes, all students receive varied instruction and will make progress. By being introduced to different types of text, students will develop skills according to their own strengths at that particular time.

33. B: Manipulatives are three-dimensional concrete objects that students can not only look at but also touch, move, dismantle and reassemble (in some cases), rearrange, etc.—i.e., manipulate as the name indicates. Examples (A) may be three-dimensional objects, demonstrations, or (more often) verbal descriptions given orally, printed, or written. Graphic organizers (C) are diagrams (e.g., Venn diagrams), charts, timelines, concept maps, word webs, etc. which are two-dimensional, visual, graphic materials. Charts, tables, and graphs (D), though less pictorial and conceptual and more linear and numerical than graphic organizers, are also two-dimensional in print, online, or on screen.

34. D: Dog, sit, leg. CVC words are composed of a consonant, a vowel, and a consonant. To learn to read them, students must be familiar with the letters used and their sounds. A teacher can present a word like *sit* to students who also know the consonants *b/f/h/p* and ask them to create a word family of other CVC words. The students will be able to read *bit, fit, hit,* and *pit* because they are similar to the word *sit* they have just learned.

35. B: Researchers find that learners of both their native language (L1) and a second language (L2) go through all three developmental stages, which means that choices A and C are both incorrect. However, learners of a second language are often urged by teachers and others to skip the Silent Period, whereas young children acquiring their native languages are not similarly expected to speak immediately. L2 learners are not likely to undergo the third stage later (D) but sooner than or at a similar time as L1 learners, due either to having not yet learned all linguistic forms of the L2 or to being unable to access all of the L2's forms as they produce language.

36. C: There is currently a wide variety of technology resources available that can support class instruction. However, teachers must choose carefully in order to ensure that the technology is useful and relevant to his or her intended learning outcomes for the class. The language lab described allows students to experience text through listening *and* reading, thereby utilizing different processes in the brain. The interactive modules also support decoding and comprehension skills that go along with the texts. This use of technology reinforces important skills in a way that will be unique and interesting for the students.

37. B: Based on Charles Read's (1975) research into invented and phonetic spelling, Richard Gentry (1982, 2006, 2010) identified five phases of spelling. *Precommunicative:* Alphabetic symbols without letter-sound correspondences, complete alphabet knowledge, spelling directionality, or uppercase and lowercase letter distinctions. *Semiphonetic:* Letter-sound correspondence understanding emerges; students frequently spell words with single letters or abbreviated syllables. *Phonetic:* Not all spellings follow standard conventions, but students systematically represent all phonemes with letters. Misspellings are typically accurate in terms of articulatory placement (*e* for short *i*, *a* for short *e*, *i* for short *o*, etc.) *Transitional:* Students move from phonetic to conventional, visual spellings, informed by their growing understanding of word structure. "Higheked" for "hiked" and "egul" for "eagle" are examples of their more approximate spellings. *Correct:* Students have learned the fundamental rules of English orthography, including irregular and alternative spellings, silent consonants, prefixes and suffixes, etc. and identify misspellings.

38. B: Understanding the meaning of words that are not familiar. Context cues offer insight into the probable meaning of unfamiliar words.

39. A: The formal version of Standard English is reflected in dictionaries and grammar books and applied in written language. In speech, Standard English is NOT universal (B): it differs in pronunciation between the northern and southern regions of North America and between native English speakers in England, Ireland, Australia, India, and other English-speaking areas. Speech communities use a more flexible variety of *informal* Standard English rather than the Standard English of writing (C). The construct of Standard English actually includes a range of dialects (D) because formal Standard English is used in writing and not speech, which by nature dictates a less formal, more flexible version.

40. C: All private and public schools will provide some sort of curriculum guidance, which usually takes the form of a list of concepts that must be covered within a certain time frame. Teachers must use this provision as a guideline for planning instruction. However, with time and creativity, teachers can bring these concepts to life using various types of material (oral, written, media, performance) and engaging instructional methods. Teachers can also find ways to integrate instruction and concepts with teachers of other subjects to ensure that students understand that language skills are not only interrelated but also applicable to all areas of learning.

41. D: Expectations include interpreting and understanding visual imagery, meanings, and messages (A); analyzing and critiquing the importance of visual media (B); and evaluating the ways that various media inform and influence people (C). Developing and organizing ideas from the environment (D) is an expectation, but *not* from the English Language Arts subject area; it is an expectation for middle school students in the Fine Arts subject area.

42. A: Closed, open, silent *e*, vowel team, vowel-*r*, and consonant-*le*. A closed syllable ends with a consonant, such as *cat*. Open syllables end with a vowel, such as *he*. Vowel team syllables contain two vowels working together, such as *main*. Vowel-*r* syllables such as *er* and *or* frequently occur as suffixes. Consonant-*le* syllables also typically occur as suffixes, such as *battle* or *terrible*.

43. C: Neologisms (from *neo-* meaning "new"), also known as "creative coinages," are new words sometimes invented by people which then become parts of our vocabulary. The word "noob" refers to a person new to a context. It was first largely used in the 1960s and 1970s to describe the new man in a military unit during the Vietnam War. Blending (A) is another way new words come into our language; for example, "moped" is a blend of the respective first syllables of "motor" and "pedal." Conversion (B), also called functional shift, changes a word's part of speech. For example, the common nouns "network," "microwave," and "fax," along with the proper noun "Google" have all been converted to verbs in modern usage. Onomatopoeia (D) means words that imitate associated sounds, such as "meow" and "click." New words are also created this way.

44. B: The teacher used an informal reading inventory to gain insight into the students' abilities in a larger group setting. While some informal reading inventories, or IRI's, are administered between one teacher and one student, these inventories usually work best in a group setting. The benefit of this type of assessment is that it provides insight within the context of an entire class or large group in a short period of time. This assessment does not provide specific or generalized information about the students' progress, but rather allows the teacher to gauge her students' needs at any given point during instruction.

45. A: Norm-referenced tests compare student scores to the average scores of a normative sample of similar students that represents the target population. Informal reading inventories (B) use graded word lists, reading passages from authentic texts, and comprehension questions to identify student reading levels, strengths, and instructional needs rather than comparing student scores to normative group scores. Curriculum-based assessments (C) test student knowledge of the specific material included in the school's curriculum rather than comparing scores. Criterion-referenced tests (D) compare student performance against pre-established criteria for mastery of specific skills, not other students' performance.

46. D: Especially important to English Language Learners and students with reading disabilities. Word recognition is required for reading fluency and is important to all readers, but it is especially so for English Language Learners and students with reading disabilities. It can be effectively taught through precisely calibrated word study instruction designed to provide readers with reading and writing strategies for successful word analysis.

47. B: When adults or other skilled readers take time to read aloud to students, they can model (or demonstrate) what it means to read fluently. Students are still learning about grammar, spelling, decoding, comprehending, speaking, and listening. Therefore, it can be difficult for them to read aloud consistently with appropriate speed, accuracy, and inflection since there are multiple cognitive processes taking place in the student's brain. By listening to an experienced reader, students will better understand how fluent reading is intended to sound and how fluency can affect comprehension in reading or listening.

48. A: The probability that the dart will land in the inner circle is equal to the ratio of the area of inner circle to the area of the outer circle, or $\frac{\pi 3^2}{\pi 6^2}$. This reduces to $\frac{1}{4}$. Therefore, the correct choice is A.

49. B: The volume of a sphere may be calculated using the formula $V = \frac{4}{3}\pi r^3$, where r represents the radius. Substituting 3.5 for r gives $V = \frac{4}{3}\pi(3.5)^3$, which simplifies to $V \approx 179.6$.

50. A: The vertical line of symmetry is represented by an equation of the form $x = a$. The horizontal line of symmetry is represented by an equation of the form $y = a$. One line of symmetry occurs at $x = -4$. The other line of symmetry occurs at $y = 6$.

51. D: To draw a box-and-whisker plot from the data, find the median, quartiles, and upper and lower limits.

```
3 | 6 7 9 9
4 | 2|3 8 8 9              Key
5 | 0|1 1 1 5|7          3 | 6 = 36
6 | 0 0 1 2 3
```

The median is $\frac{50+51}{2} = 50.5$, the lower quartile is $\frac{22+23}{2} = 22.5$, and the upper quartile is $\frac{57+60}{2} = 58.5$. The box of the box-and-whisker plot goes through the quartiles, and a line through the box represents the median of the data. The whiskers extend from the box to the lower and upper limits, unless there are any outliers in the set. In this case, there are no outliers, so the box-and-whisker plot in choice A correctly represents the data set.

To draw a pie chart, find the percentage of data contained in each of the ranges shown. There are four out of twenty numbers between 30 and 39, inclusive, so the percentage shown in the pie chart for that range of data is $\frac{4}{20} \cdot 100\% = 20\%$; there are five values between 40 to 49, inclusive, so the percentage of data for that sector is $\frac{5}{20} \cdot 100\% = 25\%$; $\frac{6}{20} \cdot 100\% = 30\%$ of the data is within the range of 50-59, and $\frac{5}{20} \cdot 100\% = 25\%$ is within the range of 60-69. The pie chart shows the correct percentage of data in each category.

Copyright © Mometrix Media. You have been licensed one copy of this document for personal use only. Any other reproduction or redistribution is strictly prohibited. All rights reserved.

To draw a cumulative frequency histogram, find the cumulative frequency of the data.

Range	Frequency	Cumulative frequency
30-39	4	4
40-49	5	9
50-59	6	15
60-69	5	20

The histogram shows the correct cumulative frequencies.

Therefore, all of the graphs represent the data set.

52. B: Since rate in mph $= \frac{\text{distance in miles}}{\text{time in hours}}$, Zeke's driving speed on the way to Atlanta and home from Atlanta in mph can be expressed as d/3 and d/2, respectively, when d=distance between Zeke's house and his destination. Since Zeke drove 20 mph faster on his way home, $\frac{d}{2} - \frac{d}{3} = 20$.

$$6\left(\frac{d}{2} - \frac{d}{3} = 20\right)$$

$$3d - 2d = 120$$

$$d = 120$$

Since the distance between Zeke's house and the store in Atlanta is 120 miles, Zeke drove a total distance of 240 miles in five hours. Therefore, his average speed was $\frac{240 \text{ miles}}{5 \text{ hours}} = 48$ mph.

53. B: All regular polygons have rotational symmetry. The angle of rotation is the smallest angle by which the polygon can be rotated such that it maps onto itself; any multiple of this angle will also map the polygon onto itself. The angle of rotation for a regular polygon is the angle formed between two lines drawn from consecutive vertices to the center of the polygon. Since the vertices of a regular polygon lie on a circle, for a regular polygon with n sides, the angle of rotation measures $\frac{360°}{n}$.

54. D: The original cost may be represented by the equation $45 = x - 0.25x$ or $45 = 0.75x$. Dividing both sides of the equation by 0.75 gives $x = 60$.

55. C: The volume of a pyramid may be calculated using the formula $V = \frac{1}{3}Bh$, where B represents the area of the base and h represents the height. Since the base is a square, the area of the base is equal to 6^2, or 36 square inches. Substituting 36 for B and 9 for h gives $V = \frac{1}{3}(36)(9)$, which simplifies to $V = 108$.

56. D: Of the available options, choice D is the most learner-centered activity since it includes hands-on activities with the use of manipulatives. Choices B and C are learner-centered but do not include hands-on activities. Choice A is teacher-centered. Therefore, the correct choice is D.

57. D: This problem can be represented using the proportion $\frac{number\ of\ wins}{total\ games} = \frac{number\ of\ wins}{total\ games}$. If the ratio of wins to losses is 2:1, then the ratio of wins to total games is 2:3. The proportion to determine the number of wins is $\frac{x}{36} = \frac{2}{3}$. Therefore, the correct choice is D.

58. B: This series lists the sum of the squares of natural numbers and 1. For example, $1^2 + 1$ is 2, and $2^2 + 1$ is 5. The next number in the series can be determined by $5^2 + 1$ which is 26. Note also that the differences between consecutive numbers in the series are consecutive odd integers starting at 3; for example, $2 + 3$ is 5, $5 + 5$ is 20, and $10 + 7$ is 17, so the next number in the series is $17 + 9$, or 26. Therefore, the correct choice is B.

59. C: Angles g and c are alternate exterior angles. Thus, they are congruent.

60. C: The numbers in this sequence progress according to a pattern. Each progressing number can be expressed by the equation x + 2 = n, where x = the difference between the previous two numbers and n = the number added to the previous number to yield the progressing number. For instance, the difference in 24 and 16 is 8. By adding 2 to 8, you know that you must add 10 to 24 in order to yield 34. In the next part of the sequence, x = 10 and n = 12. 34 + 12 = 46, the next number in the sequence.

61. D: The identity element is d since $d\#a = a\#d = a, d\#b = b\#d = b, d\#c = c\#d = c$, and $d\#d = d$. The inverse of element c is c since $c\#c = d$, the identity element. The operation # is commutative because $a\#b = b\#a, a\#c = c\#a$, etc. Rather than check that the operation is commutative for each pair of elements, note that elements in the table display symmetry about the diagonal elements; this indicates that the operation is indeed commutative.

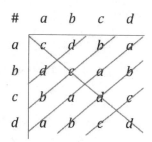

62. B: One way to approach this problem is to first consider the number of arrangements of the five members of the family if Tasha (T) and Mac (M) must sit together. Treat them as a unit seated in a fixed location at the table; then arrange the other three family members (A, B, and C):

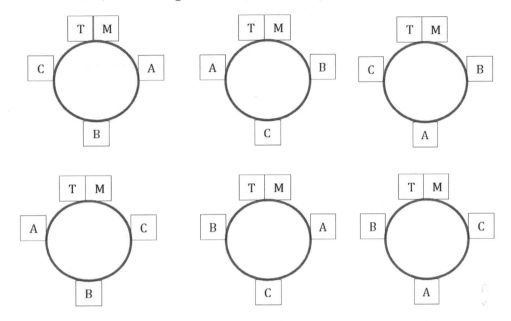

There are six ways to arrange four units around a circle as shown. (Any other arrangement would be a rotation in which the elements in the same order and would therefore not be a unique arrangement.) Note that there are $(n - 1)!$ ways to arrange n units around a circle for $n > 1$.

Of course, Mac and Tasha are not actually a single unit. They would still be sitting beside each other if they were to trade seats, so there are twelve arrangements in which the two are seated next to one another. In all other arrangements of the five family members, they are separated. Therefore, to find the number of arrangements in which Tasha and Mac are not sitting together, subtract twelve from the possible arrangement of five units around a circle: $(5 - 1)! - 12 = 12$.

63. C: A reflection across the x-axis will result in a triangle with vertices at (2, –3), (4, –7), and (6, –3). A rotation of 270 degrees is denoted by the following: $(a, b) \rightarrow (b, -a)$. Thus, a rotation of the reflected triangle by 270 degrees will result in a figure with vertices at (–3, –2), (–7, –4), and (–3, –6). The transformed triangle indeed has these coordinates as its vertices.

64. D: Real numbers include all rational and irrational numbers. Rational numbers include all integers. The set of real numbers include the other three sets. Therefore, the correct choice is D.

65. D: Congruent figures have the same shape and the same size. Two squares have the same shape. If the areas are the same, they also have the same size and are congruent. Choice A is incorrect because two rectangles can have the same perimeter but not the same shape. Choice B is incorrect because two polygons of the same shape are not necessarily the same size. Choice C is incorrect because two polygons can have the same side lengths but different shapes. Therefore, the correct choice is D.

66. C: The area of a trapezoid may be calculated using the formula, $A = \frac{1}{2}(b_1 + b_2)h$. Thus, the area of the trapezoid is represented as $A = \frac{1}{2}(4 + 2)(2)$, which simplifies to $A = 6$. The area of the triangle is represented as $A = \frac{1}{2}(4)(3)$, which also simplifies to $A = 6$. Thus, the total area is 12 square units.

67. C: The graph below shows that the lines are parallel and that the shaded regions do not overlap. There is no solution to the set of inequalities given in Choice C.

$$6x + 2y \le 12$$
$$2y \le -6x + 12$$
$$y \le -3x + 6$$
$$3x \ge 8 - y$$
$$y \ge -3x + 8$$

As in Choice C, the two lines given in Choice A are parallel; however, the shading overlaps between the lines, so that region represents the solution to the system of inequalities.

The shaded regions for the two lines in Choice B do not overlap except at the boundary, but since the boundary is same, the solution to the system of inequalities is the line $y = -2x + 6$.

Choice D contains a set of inequalities which have intersecting shaded regions; the intersection represents the solution to the system of inequalities.

68. D: The constant of proportionality is equal to the slope. Using the points, (2, −8) and (5, −20), the slope may be written as $\frac{-20-(-8)}{5-2}$, which equals −4.

69. D: Ms. Alejo is using different activities to meet the various readiness levels of her students. This aspect is described by differentiated instruction. Collaborative learning and small group instruction describe the aspect that the students are in groups. The question does not address nonlinguistic representations such as charts and visual aids. Therefore, the correct choice is D.

70. B: Graham has placed Group 1 with 40¢, Group 2 with 38¢, and Group 3 with 29¢. Henry has placed Group 1 with 34¢, Group 2 with 27¢, and Group 3 with 27¢. Landon has placed Group 1 with 59¢, Group 2 with 43¢, and Group 3 with 59¢. Elizabeth has placed Group 1 with 41¢, Group 2 with 41¢, and Group 3 with 22¢. Therefore, the correct choice is B.

71. D: The triangle is a 45-45-90 right triangle. Thus, if each leg is represented by x, the hypotenuse is represented by $x\sqrt{2}$. Thus, the hypotenuse is equal to $8\sqrt{2}$ cm.

72. C: The center of the sphere is shared by the center of the cube, and each of the corners of the cube touches the surface of the sphere. Therefore, the diameter of the sphere is the line which passes through the center of the cube and connects one corner of the cube to the opposite corner on the opposite face.

Notice in the illustration below that the diameter d of the sphere can be represented as the hypotenuse of a right triangle with a short leg measuring 4 units. (Since the volume of the cube is 64 cubic units, each of its sides measures $\sqrt[3]{64} = 4$ units.) The long leg of the triangle is the diagonal of the base of the cube. Its length can be found using the Pythagorean theorem: $4^2 + 4^2 = x^2; x = \sqrt{32} = 4\sqrt{2}$.

Use the Pythagorean theorem again to find d, the diameter of the sphere: $d^2 = \left(4\sqrt{2}\right)^2 + 4^2; d = \sqrt{48} = 4\sqrt{3}$. To find the volume of the sphere, use the formula $V = \frac{4}{3}\pi r^3$. Since the radius r of the sphere is half the diameter, $r = 2\sqrt{3}$, and $V = \frac{4}{3}\pi(2\sqrt{3})^3 = \frac{4}{3}\pi\left(24\sqrt{3}\right) = 32\pi\sqrt{3}$ cubic units.

73. C: The situation may be modeled by the system $\begin{array}{l} 4x + 3y = 9.55 \\ 2x + 2y = 5.90 \end{array}$. Multiplying the bottom equation by −2 gives $\begin{array}{l} 4x + 3y = 9.55 \\ -4x - 4y = -11.80 \end{array}$. Addition of the two equations gives $-y = -2.25$ or $y = 2.25$. Thus, one box of crackers costs $2.25.

74. B: A regular solid prism is a solid, three-dimensional shape which has length, width, and height. The bases are of the same shape, and the shape of the other faces depend on the shape of the bases. The volume of a regular solid prism can be determined by multiplying the area of the base by the height of the prism. For example, the volume of a rectangular prism is found by

$Volume = Area\ of\ base \times Height$ which is more commonly known as $Volume = Length \times Width \times Height$. Therefore, the correct choice is B.

75. D: The intersection of the two sets is empty, denoted by the symbol, ∅. There are not any elements common to both sets.

76. B: A line graph is often used to show change over time. A Venn diagram shows the relationships among sets. A box and whisker plot displays how numeric data are distributed throughout the range. A pie chart shows the relationship of parts to a whole.

Note that for class 1, the median is a better representation of the data than the mean. There are two outliers (points which lie outside of two standard deviations from the mean) which bring down the average test score. In cases such as this, the mean is not the best measure of central tendency.

77. A: Since the students are using manipulatives, this is a concrete representation. Therefore, the correct choice is A.

78. B: Since the figures are similar, the following proportion may be written and solved for x: $\frac{6}{4} = \frac{8}{x}$. Thus, $x = \frac{32}{6}$ or $5\frac{1}{3}$.

79. D: The percent increase is represented as $\frac{1100-800}{800}$, which equals 0.375 or 37.5%.

80. A: In the third line of the problem, the student incorrectly added the 5 and 2 rather than multiplying 2(2). According to the order of operations, the student should multiply before adding. Therefore, the correct choice is A.

81. B: Each of the graphs shows the correct y-intercept of –6, but only graph C shows the correct slope. Using the points (0, –6) and (–2, 2), the slope of graph B may be written as $m = \frac{2-(-6)}{-2-0}$, which simplifies to $m = -4$.

82. A: The amount to be administered may be written as $\frac{1}{12} \cdot \frac{34}{10}$, which equals $\frac{17}{60}$. Thus, she should administer $\frac{17}{60}$ fluid ounces of medicine.

83. A: Choice A correctly shows how the combination of like terms on the left side of the equation results in the expression on the right side of the equation. Choice B incorrectly combines like terms by adding the coefficients rather than subtracting. Choice C incorrectly adds the exponents of like terms instead of just adding the coefficients of like terms. Choice D incorrectly distributes the 2.5 across by parentheses by neglecting to multiply the 2.5 with the last term in the expression. Therefore, the correct choice is A.

84. B: The amount she spends on rent and utilities is equal to 0.38(40,000), or $15,200, which is approximately $15,000.

85. C: A bill is usually first reviewed by the appropriate subcommittee. The subcommittee can accept the bill, amend the bill, or reject the bill. If the subcommittee accepts or amends the bill, they send it to the full committee for review. Expert witnesses and testimony are all part of committee review.

86. B: The Virginia Company of London was based in London, not Massachusetts. It had a charter to colonize American land between the Hudson and Cape Fear rivers (C). The other Virginia Company was the Virginia Company of Plymouth, which was based in the American colony of Plymouth, Massachusetts (A). It had a charter to colonize North America between the Potomac River and the northern boundary of Maine (D). Both Virginia Companies were joint-stock companies, which had often been used by England for trading with other countries.

87. B: U.S. industrialization was confined to the Northeast until after the Civil War because the Northeast had faster-running rivers than the South. The earliest American factories used horse-drawn machines. When waterpower was developed and proved superior, the Northeast's faster rivers were more suited to water-powered mills than the South's slower rivers. The war did not delay the development of water power (A). Waterpower was developed before the Civil War in the late 1790s. Steam power, a more efficient alternative to water power, was developed after the Civil War and eventually replaced waterpower. With steam-powered engines, industry could spread to the South since steam engines did not depend on rapidly running water like water-powered engines. While British emigré Samuel Slater's first cotton mill using horse-drawn production did lose a lot of money (C), this was not a reason for industrial delay. In fact, Slater's Beverly Cotton Manufactory in Massachusetts, the first American cotton mill, in spite of its financial problems, was successful in both its volume of cotton production and in developing the water-powered technology that ultimately would succeed the horse-drawn method. Slater's second cotton mill in Pawtucket, Rhode Island, was water-powered. Industrial delay was not because milling technology had not yet been invented (D). Slater learned of new textile manufacturing techniques as a youth in England, and he brought this knowledge to America in 1789. Resistance of Southern owners of plantations and slaves did not slow the spread of industrialism. Rather, as seen in choice B above, the South did not have the geographic capability to sustain waterpower. Once steam power was developed, the South joined in industrialization.

88. D: Indentured servants agreed to work for a set period of time in exchange for transportation to the New World and such basic necessities as food and shelter. They did not receive wages and were generally not highly-educated people. Employers often viewed indentured servants with scorn and treated them as harshly as they treated slaves.

89. C: Nature imposed great hardships on farmers. Drought, wind, fires, blizzards, and subzero temperatures made life on the plains very difficult and dangerous. The invention of barbed wire in 1874 allowed farmers to keep livestock from damaging their crops. The Homestead Act of 1862 encouraged settlement of the west and made land available to some 600,000 homesteaders. Founded in 1867, the Grange united farmers in their effort to regulate storage and shipping costs and generally protect their own interests.

90. B: Southern states provided raw materials that were manufactured into commodities in Northern states. Southerners resented paying taxes to Northern states for these products (textiles, furniture, etc.).

91. A: It is not true that the founding fathers specifically stated in the Constitution that the USA would be a democracy. The founding fathers wanted the new United States to be founded on principles of liberty and equality, but they did not specifically describe these principles with the term "Democracy." Thus, the Declaration of Independence, like the Constitution after it, did not stipulate a democracy, although both did state the principles of equality and freedom (B). The Constitution also provided for the election of the new government (C), and for protection of the rights of some, but not all, of the people (D). Notable exceptions at the time were black people and women. Only later were laws passed to protect their rights over the years.

92. B: Marx's focus in *The Communist Manifesto* (1848) and *Das Kapital* (1867) was on the inevitable conflict between the working class and the capitalists who own the means of production. He identified these two opposing forces as the proletariat and the bourgeoisie.

93. A: The federal government has three branches: executive, including the President, the Vice President, and his cabinet; legislative, including the House of Representatives and the Senate; and judicial, including the Supreme Court and the court system.

94. A: By 1840, more than one-third of all Americans lived west of the Alleghenies, but not two-thirds. It is correct that in the first half of the 19th century, the American population doubled every 25 years (B). It is also correct that westward expansion increased as more people moved west (C) during these years. It is correct that there was not a lot of immigration to the U.S. from other countries before 1820 (D). It is also true that foreign immigration to America increased quickly around that time, with most immigrants coming from the British Isles.

95. D: Congress did not have the authority to levy taxes under the Articles of Confederation. Without the ability to levy taxes, there was no way to finance programs, which weakened the government.

96. D: The ancient Mayan civilization was located in what are today Guatemala, Belize, Honduras, and El Salvador in Central America and also in the Yucatan peninsula and the south of Mexico. The ancient civilization of the Incas was located in what is now Peru in South America. The ancient civilization of the Aztecs lived in what is Mexico today.

97. C: The 12th Amendment passed in 1804 gave each member of the Electoral College one vote for the President and another for the Vice President. Previously, the runner-up in the Presidential election became Vice President.

98. A: The French and Indian War (Seven Years War) 1754-1763

American Revolution 1775–1783

French Revolution 1789–1799

The War of 1812 1812-1815

99. A: The Senate and House of Representatives make up a bicameral legislature. The Great Compromise awarded seats in the Senate equally to each state, while the seats in the House of Representatives were based on population.

100. B: Lines of longitude, which run north-south from pole to pole, are used to separate time zones. Houston, Texas, and Fargo, North Dakota, which are on almost the exact same line of longitude, are both in the Central Time Zone; however, they are not in the same state, do not have the same climate, and are not equidistant from the equator. To calculate the distance from the equator, the latitude of the city would need to be known.

101. A: Choice B is a definition of gross national product, and choices C and D define other economic measures.

102. A: Representative government, by which citizens elect officials who share their views and who, in turn, present their views in a democratic system, is not a true democracy in which each individual votes on each issue. As the population of a democracy grows, the practicality of every individual voting on every issue becomes prohibitive to the process.

103. C: The Ottoman Empire joined with the Triple Alliance in 1914 as World War I began. The original Triple Alliance was formed by Austria–Hungary, Germany, and Italy in 1882 and renewed in 1902. The Ottoman Empire signed the Turco–German Alliance in August 1914, joining with the Central Powers' Triple Alliance. In October 1914, with the bombing of Russian ports on the Black Sea, Turkey formally entered World War I. The Allied Powers of the Triple Entente declared war on the Ottoman Empire in November 1914.

104. B: Article I of the Constitution mandates the taking of a census every ten years. The purpose was to be sure that each state was proportionately represented in Congress according to its population as specified in the Constitution. Census data is also used to allocate federal funding for various programs and for shaping economic policies. Individual data collected by the U.S. Bureau of the Census is kept confidential for seventy-two years and does not affect income tax rates. Every state has two seats in the Senate regardless of population.

105. C: The impact of a transaction on third parties not involved in the transaction is known as an externality. An externality can be positive, in which case it's a positive externality or social benefit. An externality can also be negative, in which case it's a negative externality or a social cost.

106. D: Ancient Greek democracy was not completely open to all of the public. However, participating persons were not chosen or excluded based on their respective socioeconomic levels. The city-state of Athens had one of the first and most well-known democracies in ancient Greece (B). It began around 500 B.C.E. (A). The experiment of Athenian democracy was unique in that it was a direct democracy, meaning people voted directly for or against proposed legislation without any representation (C) such as the House of Representatives and the Senate, as we have in modern democracies.

107. D: The Protestant work ethic is considered by many historians to have contributed to the Industrial Revolution. In Britain, where industrialization started, financial stability encouraged investment in industry; and the eventual dominance of Protestantism is believed to have contributed to a class of entrepreneurs who believed in education, technological progress, and hard work. The other choices are considered effects of industrialization: Mass production enabled the privately owned, for-profit enterprises that characterize capitalist economic systems. Socialism developed as a criticism of capitalism; Karl Marx argued that capitalism polarized societies into owners versus workers. Marx also viewed capitalism as a necessary precursor to socialism within the logical progression of economies. Romanticism also developed in reaction against mechanization, contrasting nature as more valuable in art and language versus the dark side of scientific progress.

108. C: The Underground Railroad was not necessary literally a railroad, but a series of clandestine paths to move runaway and freed slaves out of Southern States prior to 1865.

109. A: A timeline would be the best way to represent the major events of World War I. Timelines place events in chronological order, with the distance between the events correlated to their interval on the line. A timeline can run in any direction. A thematic map or a flow-line map might also be good at representing this subject, but a political map is restricted to borders and cities; therefore, it would not be able to suggest the changes caused by the war. Bar graphs and pie charts are used to depict quantities and proportions rather than sequences of events.

110. D: Resentment against the Protestant Reformation was not a cause given for the French Revolution. Choices A, B, and C are just a few among many causes cited for the war. Famines caused malnutrition and even starvation among the poorest people (A). Escalating bread prices contributed greatly to the hunger. Louis XV had amassed a great amount of debt from spending money on many wars in addition to the American Revolution. Military failures, as well as a lack of social services for veterans, exacerbated these debts. In addition, the Court of Louis XVI and Marie Antoinette spent excessively and obviously on luxuries even while people in the country were starving, and France's monetary system was outdated, inefficient, and thus unable to manage the national debt (B). Much of the populace greatly resented the Catholic Church's control of the country (C). However, there was not great resentment against the Protestant Reformation (D); there were large minorities of Protestants in France, who not only exerted their influence on government institutions, but undoubtedly also contributed to the resentment of the Catholic Church.

111. D: French chemist Louis Pasteur (1822–1895), considered one of the founders of bacteriology, developed a process of heating and cooling food products like milk and wine that reduces the number of pathogenic microbes to a level that will not cause sickness when ingested. This process is named pasteurization after him. Pasteur also made the first vaccines against both rabies and anthrax. All three of these accomplishments were incredible breakthroughs in preventing fatal diseases. Pasteur's experiments advanced the germ theory of disease, which when first proposed, met strong resistance from those who did not believe microorganisms cause sickness. His work supported its acceptance and colleague Robert Koch's proof of it in 1890. However, Pasteur did not create the first polio vaccine.

112. D: The Vice President also serves as the President of the Senate. If a tie occurs in the Senate, the Vice President casts his vote to break the tie.

113. A: Of the four answer choices, New York City is the most likely to be considered a modern cultural hearth. A cultural hearth is an area from which cultural trends emanate. Geographers suggest that there were seven original cultural hearths, including Mesoamerica and the Indus River Valley. The modes of living that originated in these areas emanated out into the rest of the world. These days, the cultural hearths tend to be the cities and countries with the most economic power. Of the four answer choices, New York City is clearly the wealthiest and the most influential. The styles and trends that originate in New York City find their way into communities all around the world.

114. A: Magnetic poles occur in pairs known as magnetic dipoles. Individual atoms can be considered magnetic dipoles due to the spinning and rotation of the electrons in the atoms. When the dipoles are aligned, the material is magnetic. Choices B, C, and D are all magnetic materials. Therefore, the magnetic dipoles in these materials are NOT randomly aligned. Only choice A has randomly aligned dipoles.

115. D: Theory. Once a hypothesis has been verified and accepted, it becomes a theory. A theory is a generally accepted explanation that has been highly developed and tested. A theory can explain data and be expected to predict outcomes of tests. A fact is considered to be an objective and verifiable observation; whereas, a scientific theory is a greater body of accepted knowledge, principles, or relationships that might explain a fact. A law is an explanation of events by which the outcome is always the same. A conclusion is more of an opinion and could be based on observation, evidence, fact, laws, or even beliefs.

116. A: Heat on Earth is generated by the Sun. The more direct sunlight an area on Earth receives from the Sun, the warmer it will be. The earth is most tilted towards or away from the sun at the solstices between spring and summer or between fall and winter. When the Northern hemisphere is tilted away from the Sun, all of the countries in the Northern hemisphere experience fall and winter. At that same time, the Southern hemisphere experiences spring and summer. The same is true when the Southern hemisphere experiences fall and winter; the Northern hemisphere experiences spring and summer.

117. C: At carrying capacity. A population that reaches maximum size and ceases to grow due to a limited availability of resources is said to be at carrying capacity. The carrying capacity of a species is influenced by many factors such as the amount of land or water available, food supply and predators. Unstable and moving towards extinction are not correct as carrying capacity does not necessarily mean it is unstable or becoming extinct. Shrinking exponentially is also incorrect as the question says it has stopped growing, not that it is reducing in size.

118. A: The center of an atom is known as the nucleus. It is composed of protons and neutrons.

119. C: 20 g/L. One way to measure the density of an irregularly shaped object is to submerge it in water and measure the displacement. This is done by taking the mass (40 grams), then finding the volume by measuring how much water it displaces. Fill a graduated cylinder with water and record the amount. Put the object in the water and record the water level. Subtract the difference in water levels to get the amount of water displaced, which is also the volume of the object. In this case, 4.5

liters minus 2.5 liters equals 2 liters. Divide mass by volume (40 grams divided by 2 liters) to get 20 g/L (grams per liter).

120. A: high solubility in water. Most organic molecules have all of the following properties except high solubility in water. A tendency to melt, covalently bonded, and high flammability are all characteristics of organic molecules. Organic molecules are those that contain carbon molecules, with a few exceptions. Organic molecules tend to be less soluble in water than inorganic salts. They are good at forming unique structures and there are many organic compounds. Examples of organic compounds include hydrocarbons, carbohydrates, lipids, and proteins.

121. D: Heat. The formation of sedimentary rock does not include heat. Of the three types of rock igneous, sedimentary and metamorphic, heat is essential to two: igneous and metamorphic. Sedimentary rocks are formed by sediments that get deposited and then compacted or cemented together. Sedimentary rocks are classified into detrital, organic or chemical sediments. Layering is correct since sediments can be deposited or otherwise formed in layers. Cementation is also called lithification. Compaction refers to the pressure forming sedimentary rock leading to cementation.

122. A: Descriptive studies are usually the first form of study in a new area of scientific inquiry. Others are also forms of scientific study but are completed after initial descriptive studies.

123. A: It takes half the amount of energy to increase the temperature of a 1 kg sample of ice by 1°C than a 1 kg sample of water. Heat capacity refers to the amount of heat or thermal energy required to raise the temperature of a specific substance a given unit. A substance with a higher heat capacity requires more heat to raise its temperature than a substance with a lower heat capacity. The comparison here is that the specific heat capacity of ice is half as much as that of liquid water, so it takes half the amount of energy to increase the same amount of ice one temperature unit than it would if it were liquid water.

124. A: The molecular arrangement is random in some directions and regular in others. This best describes the molecular arrangement of a liquid crystal. A liquid crystal may seem like a contradiction as it seems to refer to two different states of matter. Liquid crystals have properties of both liquids and solids. The molecules of a liquid crystal are loosely bound allowing them to flow, like a liquid, yet they arrange themselves in a repeating pattern, like the molecules of a solid which are rigidly fixed in a pattern. Liquid crystals can also organize into layers, but with randomness in the layers.

125. A: It compares the amount of radioactive material in a rock to the amount that has decayed into another element. This best describes the process of absolute dating. Choice B is not usually done. Usually, the stratigraphic layer of rock is used to date the fossils, referred to as relative dating. Choice C is incorrect as this would not lead to a correct date since the daughter elements may have a different half-life than the parent material.

126. A: The scientific method is a series of steps to solve a problem. Choices B, C, and D are all parts of the scientific method.

127. A: Enzymes are large protein molecules that act as biological catalysts and play an important role in all bodily processes. They are not fat soluble, are not acids, and are not lipids. Therefore, choice A is correct.

128. B: A reaction that uses electricity to drive it. An electrolysis reaction is a chemical reaction that uses electricity to drive it. Electrolysis reactions take place in an electrolytic cell where one substance will be oxidized and another will be reduced using electrical energy from a battery or other source. Usually, an electrolytic cell is made up of a battery connected to two metal electrodes which are placed in two separate ionic solutions. A salt bridge connects the two beakers of solution and allows positive or negative ions to flow into the solutions as needed to keep the charge balanced as the reaction takes place. The electrode where oxidation takes place is called the anode, which would be connected to the negative terminal on a battery. The electrode where reduction takes place is called the cathode and is connected to the positive terminal of a battery. These reactions are very important for electroplating metals.

129. D: Phase of the Moon. Ocean currents are not controlled by the phase of the moon. The phases of the moon refer to our viewpoint from Earth of the sun's illumination of the moon. Half the moon is illuminated by the sun at any given time. For example, a new moon is one we do not see because the side being lit by the sun is not facing us. The revolution of the moon around the earth affects the ocean tides, providing two highs and two lows at any given point during the day. Wind affects the surface currents of the ocean. Landmasses affect ocean currents as well. Earth's rotation affects the deep currents.

130. C: The majority of the solar energy that reaches Earth is absorbed by the oceans, which make up 71 percent of the Earth's surface. Because of water's high specific heat capacity, oceans can absorb and store large quantities of heat, thus preventing drastic increases in the overall atmospheric temperature.

131. B: Farther from. Electrons with greater amounts of energy are found farther from the nucleus than electrons with less energy. The principle quantum number describes the level or shell that an electron is in. The lower the number, the closer the electron is to the nucleus and the lower it is in energy.

132. C: meiosis I. In humans, diploid cells are those that contain 46 chromosomes. There are 23 pairs of chromosomes each made up of one chromosome from the father and one from the mother. In meiosis I, each chromosome replicates itself and lines up, or synapses, with its homologous chromosome, and each of the daughter cells ends up with one copy of each of the chromosomes. The two daughter cells at the end of meiosis I are haploid because they contain half of the chromosomes of the parent cell. In humans, this would be 23 chromosomes. However, each of these chromosomes is made of two sister chromatids. In meiosis II, the sister chromatids in the daughter cells separate and result in the production of the gametes. These are also haploid cells because they contain one copy of half of the genetic material of the parent cell. Four haploid cells result from meiosis. Mitosis refers to the process of cell division where each daughter cell contains exactly the same genetic material as the parent cell. Telophase refers to phases of both mitosis and meiosis, during which chromosomes move toward the opposite ends of the cell.

133. B: Land breeze. When land cools off rapidly at night and the ocean water stays relatively warm, it creates a land breeze. Sea breeze, or onshore breeze, occurs when the land heats the air above it. This heated, warmer air is less dense and rises. The cooler air from above the sea and higher sea level pressure creates a wind flow in the direction of the land. Coastal areas often have these cooler breezes. A monsoon is a seasonal wind in southern Asia that blows southwest in one season and northeast in another. The southwest winds in the summer bring heavy rain. The trade winds are the steady easterlies about the equator.

134. A: The structure of the Milky Way galaxy is spiral, meaning it has curved "arms" stretching out from a central point. While spiral galaxies have a flat, disc-like appearance, elliptical galaxies are three-dimensional and appear to be roughly the same shape regardless of the viewing angle.

135. C: The ball will move forward with respect to the boat. Newton's first law of motion states that an object in motion tends to stay in motion until a force acts to change it. The ball is initially at rest with respect to the boat, but the boat is moving forward. When the front of the boat hits the dock, the boat quickly decelerates, but the ball does not. It continues to move forward because the force acting to stop the boat does not significantly affect the ball. With the ball now moving forward faster than the boat, the ball's motion relative to the boat is forward motion.

136. B: Family. Organisms that belong to the same taxonomic group of family are most alike. In biological taxonomy, the ranks in descending order are Life, Domain, Kingdom, Phylum, Class, Order, Family, Genus, and Species. The ranks become more exclusive and specific as the classification descends. Phylum, class, and order are all higher than the family group. The higher the rank, the fewer requirements it takes to be a member. Two mnemonics for taxonomy are Kings Play Cards On Fat Green Snakes or King Philip Cuts Open Five Green Snakes.

137. B: It will ensure the health and safety of populations and the long-term sustainability of the environment. Recycling and using alternative sources of energy reduce the amount of pollutants introduced into the ecosystem, reduce the potential for disease-related human maladies, and reduce the reliance on non-renewable resources. Greater production of goods and consumer spending in the future would probably be good for the economy, but not necessarily the environment. Fossil fuels are considered to be a non-renewable energy resource.

138. C: Venus is not a gas giant. The four gas giants are Jupiter, Saturn, Uranus, and Neptune. While these "gas giants" are larger than Earth and are comprised mostly of gasses, Venus is a terrestrial planet that is comparable in size to the Earth.

139. B: Choice D would violate the law of conservation of energy. If the chemicals heat up, their temperatures increase, and their kinetic energies therefore increase, so energy could not have been obtained from kinetic energy, so choice A is incorrect. Nor do chemical reactions typically involve absorption of heat from the environment as stated by choice C: Choice B correctly describes the situation: chemical bonds contain some amount of potential energy, which may be released in certain chemical reactions.

140. D: Carbon dioxide and water. Respiration produces carbon dioxide and water. The net equation of respiration is the reverse of the equation for photosynthesis. Respiration is a series of reactions that consume glucose and oxygen to release energy and produce carbon dioxide and water. Oxygen and glucose are the substances that are broken down in respiration.

Thank You

We at Mometrix would like to extend our heartfelt thanks to you, our friend and patron, for allowing us to play a part in your journey. It is a privilege to serve people from all walks of life who are unified in their commitment to building the best future they can for themselves.

The preparation you devote to these important testing milestones may be the most valuable educational opportunity you have for making a real difference in your life. We encourage you to put your heart into it—that feeling of succeeding, overcoming, and yes, conquering will be well worth the hours you've invested.

We want to hear your story, your struggles and your successes, and if you see any opportunities for us to improve our materials so we can help others even more effectively in the future, please share that with us as well. **The team at Mometrix would be absolutely thrilled to hear from you!** So please, send us an email (support@mometrix.com) and let's stay in touch.

If you feel as though you need additional help, please check out the other resources we offer:

Study Guide: http://mometrixstudyguides.com/PraxisII

Flashcards: http://mometrixflashcards.com/PraxisII